HillBilly

Lessons for the Road

STUFF THEY NEVER TAUGHT YOU AT SCHOOL

Billy Roberts

Copyright © 2025 Billy Roberts.

All rights reserved.

ISBN: 978-0-6459142-6-9 eBook
ISBN: 978-0-6459142-7-6 Paperback

Other Books by the Author:

CROSSROADS - Rugby League's Greatest Battle

Contents

Intro. 1
All positions in life are temporary 4
Awareness is to the mind what light is to a dark room 7
Know thyself. 10
Begin with the end in mind. 13
Discipline. 16
Decisions 21
Read and never stop learning. 25
Set your navigation system 29
Attitude, the magic word 31
We become what we think about. 34
Every failure or adversity carries a seed of equivalent advantage. 37
Rediscovery of practice 40
Don't watch what people say, watch what they do 42
Become a person of value, not importance. 44
We have everything we need 47
Our higher mental faculties. 49
Create and produce. 52
Know the truth. 55
Get the facts. 57
Questions. 59
Emotions rule the world 62
Destroy what holds you in slavery 64
Time is finite, work is infinite 68
The Eisenhower Decision Matrix. 71
Time is not measured by a clock 76
Don't water last year's crops. 79

You're either growing or dying	82
Resistance always comes	85
Feelings follow actions	87
Calmness	89
Focus on contribution and service first	91
There is no luck, only causes	93
Knowledge is experience	96
Environment is more important than heredity	99
The only security comes from within	101
Riches come in two forms	103
Money is just a magnifying glass	106
Straight satisfy thyself of the truth	108
Total focus	110
One hour a day	113
Fear is your greatest enemy	115
Procrastination is the second greatest enemy	118
Ego - man's Achilles heel	121
Stop doing list	124
The wisdom to do nothing	127
Quitting is a skill	130
Multiple identities	133
Know where you are - keep score	136
Gratitude	140
Give graciously and without fanfare	143
Discontent can be healthy	145
If you don't like it, change it - you're not a tree	147
Change, the remedy for an anxious and worried mind	149
Peace of mind - develop yourself fully is the only way	152
Excellence	154
Turn disgust into inspiration	157
Confidence comes from knowledge	160
Dealing with uncertainty	162
All problems are temporary	168
Having options	171
Creative thinking	174
Take risks	176
We all need adventure	178

Always have something to look forward to............... 181
Everything which ever has been and ever will be is here now and can be discovered 183
Character must be your foundation.................. 185
Courage - the finest of all values 188
Integrity - the number one quality for success and happiness . 191
Leadership 194
Lead by example, judge by results 196
Communication 198
Listening 200
Forgive.. 202
Friendships...................................... 204
Social fitness..................................... 207
Hobbies 210
We need others................................... 212
Helping others 215
Association...................................... 217
Chase people's needs, not your wants.................. 219
Responsibility and duty............................ 221
Suffering.. 223
Find meaning and purpose 226
Numbers and likes 230
Stimulation can drive you 233
Focus on the process, not the event................... 235
Motivation over enforced discipline.................. 237
Everything is energy 241
Mental paradigms................................. 244
The world we look for.............................. 247
The pursuit of happiness can only come from the happiness of pursuit 249
Total commitment 253
Meeting the right partner 255
Finances.. 259
Good health..................................... 265
Self care 267
Develop your style 269
The horsemen of the mind 272

Look to this one day only 274
Every morning you come alive again 276
Think on death. 277
Keep bouncing 279
Carry the fire 281
Follow your own path. 283
Epitaph - your legacy 285
Epilogue. 287

Intro

The teacher will appear when the student is ready

I came out of school not knowing much. I loved rugby league, cricket, music, travel, fishing and hunting, but none of those were ever going to be a viable professional career option for me after high school. I hated high (senior) school and found I did not fit in with the structured learning environment or education curriculum. The classroom bored me to death and I found none of it relevant and was totally unprepared for life after school.

I left school after just one day in Year 11 at age sixteen. All my mates had taken trade jobs in the summer holidays and I was left on my own when I returned the following year. I quickly took the first job I could find, much to my parents' disgust and urging, when they did not want me lying around home all day.

This decision was the first of many mistakes I would make on my personal journey, and unfortunately, I had many more painful lessons to learn on this adventure of life, as I lacked both the knowledge and wisdom at that period to be successful or valuable.

My first job at sixteen in a bearing shop was one I quickly realised I hated and was not suited for at all. I stuck it out for a few years before having a fight with the boss and quitting on the spot.

Over the next two decades plus, I would go through an epiphany or what you might call finally receiving a real school of life education in the philosophies, beliefs, truths, attitudes, thoughts, character traits, decisions and disciplines that would be needed to live a successful and adventurous life.

The quote that "The teacher will appear when the student is ready" was certainly true for me, and that teacher was life itself.

There were many highs and lows, successes and failures on this adventure, from being broke, unemployed, having no idea what I wanted to do with my life, moving cities and states, working in jobs I hated, relationship failures, business failures and the inner emotional war of fear, worry, doubt and regret that we all must fight against constantly.

Despite the many failures mentioned, the successes far outweigh the disappointments, and, as Cervantes famously said, "The journey is better than the end." The Journey of Adventure: achievement, striving, finding more meaning and purpose, knowing the truths, destroying bad habits, becoming a greater being, giving, growing and reaching new levels of personal growth that I once could never imagine is one I urge all readers to aspire to, no matter where you are at in life.

Intro

This crazy adventure that I went through after quitting my first job has now been distilled into what I call HillBilly Lessons for the Road. These are some of the best lessons I have learned and I wished I knew many of them before I left school after just one day in Year 11, or in my early twenties when I made mistake after mistake. These philosophies, lessons, or laws, as I call them, will change your life and help you reach the next level of whatever you are trying to achieve in any endeavour or field.

HillBilly Lessons for the Road came from a variety of sources, such as many books, great teachers (many who I never met), conversations, extensive travelling, failure and success, finding the real truths, and my own personal experiences from an adventurous life. I pass these on to you and hope they will impact and benefit your life like they have done mine. I wish you success, adventure and happiness on your own journey.

Billy Roberts

All positions in life are temporary

Change is constant

Wherever you are is fine, only your direction is critical
- William E Bailey

Up, down or sideways, things will change

If you change, everything will change
- Jim Rohn

One of the foundational laws of life is that all positions in life are temporary and change is constant throughout one's life, from birth to death.

"Nothing stands still on this spinning planet and we must learn the importance of change and how nothing will last forever and harness this for our own good."

I first heard this quote from personal development leader and Jim Rohn's mentor, William E Bailey in his great book of poetry, *The Rhythms of Life,* and it hit me hard because it was the utter truth. You know the truth when you hear it, and Bailey's quote was spot on!

I reflected that every position in my life had been temporary and there was certain to be more change ahead in the future.

I, like so many others, had seen tremendous change in my own life, from my age changing every year, leaving school, changing jobs and careers, my health going up and down, being broke and then having surplus cash, moving across many towns and states, having people come in and out of my life, and starting out in life with ignorance and moving towards knowledge and understanding.

I could look back and see tremendous change, and I am sure you can too if you look back at your own life. You could even look at the rapid change the world has seen over the last century, with television, radio, computers, smartphones, internet, major wars and conflicts, the Great Depression, the collapse of the USSR, the Holocaust, the fall of the Berlin wall, September 11, JFK's assassination, women's rights, cars, planes and many other inventions and events changing the world around us. Just look at the incredible change in the world since March 2020 with the pandemic.

Take a look at a common path for many women, which starts at childhood, to teenager, to a working career, marriage, kids, to finally being a grandparent and then death. This example could be applied to anyone's life and is proof that change is constant and all positions in life are temporary.

Many folks see change as a negative and are fearful of any form of change today. The thought of change scares millions to death, be it changing jobs, moving to a new town, starting a business, asking a girl out, or any other change that will force a person to get out of his or her comfort zone.

The law that all positions in life are temporary is both a warning to the rich and a word of hope to the poor, as nothing lasts forever.

If we know that there has been change in our past, we can be certain that there will be more changes in our future.

"Change" is another word for opportunity, and we must use this law to our advantage and steer with our choices towards the grand life we envision for ourselves and our families and not be caught standing still with the world changing around us.

There have been plenty of times in my life where the position I found myself in was not good, from having no money, no job, and epic failures that had me down, but I stood on solid ground or held onto a universal law, knowing that all positions in life were temporary and I could change the direction for my life.

Wherever you are in life is fine, only your direction is critical, is a philosophy that has been a foundation for my life and a tremendous source of encouragement.

All positions in life are temporary: Knowing that is both a letter of hope and a warning to us all to ensure we use change to our advantage, because it will be constant throughout all our lives. Pick the changes you want for your life rather than let them come along and happen anyway.

Awareness is to the mind what light is to a dark room

The more you know, the more you can see and do

Awareness is the first step on your road to greatness

It all starts with awareness

I was in an indoor swimming pool in Cork, Ireland a number of years back, when I engaged an attractive Irish girl in conversation who was doing laps beside me at the pool. She quickly recognised my thick Australian accent and we got into a light conversation. She asked me where I had been on this trip and where else I planned to travel and visit whilst in Ireland. I told her of my itinerary and future plans. She then asked me, "Are you not going to Dingle?"

I said, "No, I have actually never heard of the place!" She was stunned and said I must change my trip plans immediately and go see Dingle, as I was only a few short hours away by car and it was the most gorgeous little place in Ireland, and there was also a stunning coastline drive on the Dingle Peninsula that was famous with both locals and tourists.

After we finished our conversation, I went back to my room and did some research on Dingle and quickly saw the many rave reviews for the region. I immediately cancelled my existing plans and booked three nights in the little village of Dingle.

Dingle and the Dingle Peninsula was everything and more that the girl had promised and is still one of my favourite places in all of Ireland and Europe to this day. That one short conversation left memories that will now last a lifetime.

Dingle had always been there; it was in major travel books, travel shows and across the internet, and yet I had no clue because I had no awareness that it even existed.

That is the power of awareness, when you go from not knowing to becoming aware, and it is one of the most powerful laws you can learn.

Most people go through life in a state of not knowing, and pay huge consequences for such ignorance and often arrogance. We conform or blindly follow the modern-day influences of legacy media, social media, news content and the people we interact with on a daily basis, who often have less awareness than ourselves and are also blindly following the crowd or conforming.

Awareness is the first step on your road to personal growth and discovery: becoming aware that you can change and that your past does not control your future and that there are much better ways of living. Awareness is the beginning of living a better life.

The gaining of knowledge and awareness is a process that we all must diligently seek out, and it is one of the first steps to change and growth.

Awareness can improve our lives in ways we could never imagine, from how to earn more money, get healthier and fitter, become more knowledgeable, have better relationships, achieve more, perform our jobs better, be a better communicator and leader, become a successful entrepreneur and investor, have more adventures and see more of the world, or anything we could imagine to improve or change in our own lives.

Today, in the information age, with so much misinformation, it is more critical than ever before that we become aware of the truth.

Awareness turns the lights up in our world, helps us see and know more, and protects us from the wrong influences. We must continually seek it out to live a great life. The cost of not seeking it out means living a life in ignorance, which will cost us dearly in more ways than one.

Awareness is to the mind what light is to a dark room and is our starting point to personal transformation.

Know thyself

To thine own self be true
- Shakespeare (Hamlet, Act I, Scene 3)

Once you really get to know yourself,
you will find you're quite the person

Who am I?

Know thyself
- Socrates

The unexamined life is not worth living
- Socrates

Authenticity in an age of influencers and
wanna be stars is so refreshing

Greek philosopher Socrates was one of the first great thinkers of antiquity and his motto was "Know thyself!" Sadly, that astute piece of wisdom now, over some 2,000 years ago from when it was first written down, is rarely taught or learned in the modern education system or at home. We sadly go through our life not really knowing who we are as individuals.

Knowing who and what we are and what we like and dislike, what our passions are and what gives us energy is one of the great laws we all must learn if we are to truly live an authentic and happy life — not becoming what family and friends think we should do, what the media sells or the education system preaches — as Friedrich Nietzche said, becoming who we are.

This undertaking of really knowing myself was a very painful process for me. As mentioned, I left school at sixteen with little knowledge, skills or understanding of what I wanted to do with my life, and, at that time, I had no clue who I really was and what made me tick or excited me and what I was naturally gifted with and suited for.

This lesson became very apparent in my late twenties when I was working with a state government agency in industrial relations, which included duties such as dealing with disputes and grievances, enterprise bargaining negotiations and commission hearings for a wide range of workplace matters. It struck me one day, after being in the role for a few years and talking with colleagues who seemed to have much more passion for the work than I did, that I did not like this kind of work, nor did I have any genuine passion for it, despite the fact it was a well-paying career with great employment conditions.

Just as I had learned in my first job at sixteen in the bearing shop, I realised I did not like this type of work. I found it to be boring, too bureaucratic, and energy sapping, there were colleagues who I did not enjoy working with, and the longer I stayed in that type of work, the more uninterested, unsuited and less motivated I became. When you have no drive or energy to get up in the morning and you go to work consistently with those feelings, something is trying to tell you that you are on the wrong path, and that was my case, for sure.

Knowing thyself is a process that we all must undertake if we are to stop following the crowd, leave conformity behind and live an authentic and true life, and become who we really are.

It is one we must explore with inner reflection and learn through experience, as we move through life's many stages and phases.

Reflection and actual experience were the strategies I utilised to really get to know myself and what I wanted to do with my life. It did not happen overnight but was a process that took many, many years and is one that still continues today.

The inner reflection was about what sort of work I like and did not like, what made me happy, did I like working with people or making things, did I like living in the country or bigger cities, which countries did I love to travel to, what girls had the right qualities as a long-time partner, whose friendships did I enjoy that added great benefit to both parties, what style of music, favourite literature and authors, favourite sports, favourite foods and restaurants, what hobbies brought the best out of me, what gave me great energy and drive, and what were my inner thoughts and beliefs on many matters.

Knowing thyself is hard work, but it has a tremendous reward and ensures you are living your best life and being truly authentic to both yourself and others. That is one of the highest honours we can all aspire to in life.

Begin with the end in mind

I dream my painting and then I paint my dream
- Vincent Van Gogh

You become your goals
- Earl Nightingale

*Definite of purpose is the starting point
from which one must begin*
- Napoleon Hill

*Anything the mind can conceive
and believe it can achieve*
- Napoleon Hill

All architects, artists and creative types commence with the end in mind before they start any project. Vincent Van Gogh said, "I dream my painting and then I paint my dream," and we must do the same with designing our own lives.

Our life is a blank canvas and each of us begins at the starting block, often with nothing more than our hopes, dreams and a burning ambition to make something of our lives. The fabulous thing is, we can design the life we want for ourselves no matter where we are, what stage of life we find ourselves at or no matter how bad or good our position may be.

Without a goal or dream, we are restless creatures who drift aimlessly through life with no clear direction or destination, and in many ways go backwards fast without some grand goal that stirs our soul with passion, energy and drive. The worst thing about not having big goals is that we waste our time with frivolous things that have no meaning or importance.

Beginning with the end in mind must be a foundation for our lives, knowing what we want and what work we must do to make it become a reality, designing the life we want and not what others think or the modern influences of social media and legacy media that hold people back from living an authentic life. We should take some time to really listen to our inner thoughts and desires to know what really stirs emotions and energy and makes us come alive.

Napoleon Hill said the number one key to success for any individual was to first ensure they have definiteness of purpose about what they want in life. Hill said anything that the mind can conceive and believe, it can achieve. Without being definite and making a firm decision about what we want from our lives, we just drift and never go on to achieve what we really want, and often get the things in life we don't want, which has become all too common for many around the world.

Beginning with the end in mind is a constant process and we often need re-creation and destruction to determine what we want through various stages in our lives.

Begin with the end in mind and design the life you want with your vocation, finances, health, relationships, adventures, learning, causes you wish to support, and personal things.

Setting goals will lead to a life of enjoyment, fulfilment and happiness, and ensure that you do not waste your life or conform or become a follower on the road that only leads to misery and unhappiness, from drifting and from not making firm decisions.

School and work don't teach anything about beginning with the end in mind, but without knowing what we want in life, we will only drift and never find our heart's desires.

Set some big goals and pursue them with great drive and persistence. Always begin with the end in mind!

Discipline

*Discipline is the bridge between
thought and accomplishment*
- Jim Rohn

Do the thing and you shall have the power
- Ralph Waldo Emerson

Through discipline comes freedom
- Aristotle

Personal development legend Jim Rohn once said that we all must suffer one of two pains: the pain of discipline or the pain of regret. He went on to say that discipline weighs ounces while regret weighs tons — brutally honest and truthful words that have stood on the concrete of truth throughout the ages and are a great warning to all to follow the straight and narrow road rather than living a life of leisure and pleasure that will end in great pain and regret.

To live a successful life, discipline must be the key foundation of your character and daily habits. Without discipline, you're in for a world of pain and disappointment. With it, the opportunities are endless, and it can be the foundation that holds our lives together, no matter what the storms of life may bring.

It's counterintuitive, but discipline leads to personal freedom, whilst the undisciplined loose life leads to chains of despair and addictions of all kinds. Are people who have all sorts of bad habits and addictions free? Of course not, as only discipline can lead to freedom.

Aristotle said, "We are what we repeatedly do," but too often those habits are time wasting and tension relieving rather than disciplines that will bring joy, pride and happiness into our lives.

There is no doubt it is getting harder and harder to develop discipline, with so many distractions in the digital age that are designed to be addictive.

The absence of discipline is one of the key reasons why so few lead successful lives. The enemy of discipline is procrastination, putting off today for tomorrow or the next day what really should be done today.

Procrastination has been one of my greatest enemies. It has destroyed millions of lives around the world. It seems nothing to put off something for a day or two, but over a lifetime, this attitude and habit will destroy our lives, as we reach the end with regret and disappointment. The compounding effect of either good or bad daily habits leads to completely different directions and destinations for our lives. As Einstein said, "Compound interest is the 8th wonder of the world," when you realise just how powerful it really is.

As Jim Rohn said, "What is easy to do is also easy not to do." It's easy to walk around the block every day or eat well but it's also easy not to do those things.

Discipline is not the easiest trait to learn or incorporate into our daily lives. With so much of the modern world at our fingertips or on a screen, developing this classic and virtuous trait is not as easy as it once was or ingrained into our youthful years like it was in bygone times.

Very few environments really teach or develop discipline today, with the schooling system silent on the subject and few parents teaching this to children at home.

It was not a subject I received much of an education on, and for many years, I paid a heavy price for my lack of discipline and procrastination. A few still do incorporate this subject, though, such as the military, elite sporting organisations or high-performing environments that really demand consistency, and those individuals that come out of these environments often have a huge advantage in life over many who struggle with focus and having discipline.

Developing discipline and the habits of success and happiness must be the foundation of your life. Discipline and developing good habits are also the quickest way to a healthy self esteem, no matter what age or sex you are. You just feel so much better when you do the work that needs to be done on a daily basis, but you feel the complete opposite when you procrastinate and put off what needs to be done today. It really does impact our mindset. The idle and unemployed are often the unhappiest in society.

Discipline

Today's psychologists and mental health practitioners rarely talk about discipline and the role it plays in a person's self esteem and just feeling bloody good. High self esteem is one of the best side effects from our daily discipline, but it gets hardly any discussion in the media or anywhere. The lack of it erodes our psyche and makes us feel and think badly.

Too often, we look at the end result we want and forget the daily habits and disciplines required to reach our goals and dreams: those nitty gritty daily habits that must be completed day after day, month after month, year after year.

Great health, strong relationships, a successful career, a thriving business, financial independence, healthy families, knowledge, a unique lifestyle and skills all take time to build. They are a process of daily consistencies rather than a one-off event, as is so often portrayed in movies and modern culture.

Developing good habits and discipline is becoming aware of the need for constant and intelligent activity on a daily basis. Endless knowledge and information is useless without action. If we don't apply what we read and learn, it will make no difference whatsoever at the end.

If we develop and practise daily disciplines, we can change our health, income, relationships, knowledge base, lifestyle, attitudes or anything else that we wish to change. Often, the only ingredient missing to change these areas or the direction of our lives is discipline!

The choice to be disciplined or procrastinate is ours, but be warned — it will either lead to great regret or success in our lives as we move through the years.

Develop healthy habits and make discipline the foundation and bedrock of your life. With discipline as your foundation, you are ensuring your life is built on rock and not sand.

Decisions

Your decisions become your destiny

You have the power to design and live the life you want and it all starts with a single decision

I am where I am because of the choices I made, and that is as true for you as it is for me -
- HillBilly saying

Decisions are the greatest dormant power within humans

One of the greatest powers that lie within each of us is the power of decisions.

Sadly, hardly any person receives any proper teaching or training on how to make decisions and reap the benefits of this powerful force. Instead, we waste this great power, as it lies dormant within each of us.

I was never taught the power of decision-making in school, in the family home or in the workplace, and have seen the consequences of this throughout my life when one does not make a firm decision. In the workplace today, so many leaders cannot make a decision. Staff watch on with frustration and anger as the boss procrastinates. The guy likes a girl and yet wastes time and she loses interest if he never has the courage to ask her out. People complain about all their problems but never do anything to change their life or situation, when all it often takes is a single decision to change direction.

Decisions can be life changing and they hold tremendous power for both good or bad. Our choices can lead us to the life we desire or to total destruction from within and a life we don't want.

One of the greatest threats and enemies you will face on the road of life is procrastination, the complete opposite of making a firm decision. Procrastination does not seem like much of an issue if you put something off for a few days, but with a lifetime of this deadly habit, your life will be destroyed and you will look back in time with heavy regret of what might have been.

As stated above, no one ever taught me the power of making firm decisions and I paid a heavy price in my early working career. Some of the most important decisions you and I are called on to make in life occur between the ages of 18 to 25, which no one ever warned me about. These can include: what career to pursue, where to live, whether to go to university or get a trade, whether to get married, whether to buy a house or car, and how much debt to take on. Many more of life's big questions are required to be made early in life, and most people don't have the wisdom or awareness to make successful decisions so early.

But that's okay, because we can turn everything to good with the power of making better decisions. I can testify to the truth of this.

Decisions

Many times, I have changed the direction of my life, from quitting jobs I hated, to moving to new places and states I liked and was more suited to, ending relationships that were becoming toxic, removing myself from emotional vampires, having a more adventurous life and finding financial security.

It all starts with decisions. Everything we desire from this life is only a decision away, and we must make full use of the great power of making decisions.

What health do we want, where do we want to live, what career would be most satisfying, what would we like to give and share, where would we like to travel to, would we like to meet our ideal partner, what does financial independence or wealth look like? These are just a few questions that are all possible when we make a firm decision to change course.

A single decision can totally change the direction of our lives. We may not reach the destination or end goal immediately, but we can move onto the right track and change our direction.

It seems often that the forces of life will try to push and pull us back to a mediocre existence. We must resist this at all costs. It all starts with making well informed and deliberate decisions as to the direction we really want for our lives and families.

Welcome all negative emotions such as disgust, frustration and regret, as they can be powerful triggers to find new inspiration and energy.

The power to decide has the power to change our lives and take us to higher levels that we never thought possible. It is one of the greatest God-given powers we each have in our personal arsenal to navigate life. So let's use it to our advantage.

Read and never stop learning

You'll be the same person in five years as you are today except for the people you meet and the books you read
- Charlie Tremendous Jones

Knowledge is to your future as light is to a dark room
- William E Bailey

Get wisdom and understanding
- Solomon in the Bible (Proverbs 4:7)

Reading and acquiring knowledge on a regular basis is essential if we wish to live the good life and find out and explore all that is available around the world.

Many of the greats from both the present and the past had one thing in common, that they were avid readers: Shakespeare, Aristotle, John Steinbeck, Jane Austen, Ralph Waldo Emerson, Henry David Thoreau, Teddy Roosevelt, Abraham Lincoln, George Orwell, Ayn Rand, JR Tolkien, Jack London, CS Lewis, F Scott Fitzgerald, Cormac McCarthy, George Patton, Douglas MacArthur, George Washington, Benjamin Franklin, Thomas Jefferson, Alexander Hamilton, John Adams, Ernest Hemingway, Winston Churchill,

Albert Einstein, Bruce Lee, Earl Nightingale, Jim Rohn and many more.

Books were the energy and fuel that would drive them to dazzling heights and open up all sorts of possibilities and ideas for their future.

It wasn't until I was in my mid-twenties that I would become an avid reader. At school, I hated English or reading books, with the only exceptions being rugby league, music, hunting and cricket magazines. Not being a reader would result in massive pain during my twenties, and I quickly learned from one of our previous laws that awareness is to the mind like light is to a dark room, and what you don't know does indeed hurt you.

I'm not sure what really set off my desire to become a voracious reader. I think I found myself in a bad position in life and falling behind and needing answers to get me out of my current predicament. Necessity has been known to be the mother of invention, and there is certainly some truth to that.

Some of the key reasons why I achieved very little up to my mid-twenties are: (1) I was not aware, (2) I had no knowledge or conception of what was possible, and (3) I was not stimulated. This was all due to not being a reader, which cost me dearly in those early years when I could have saved myself from tremendous pain and made far more progress.

Read and never stop learning

How can you achieve and make progress if you are not aware, have no knowledge and are not stimulated? You simply can't, as I learned in my early twenties.

Reading and the gaining of knowledge opens up all sorts of possibilities to our lives and futures.

It's like a painter, who at one time had only one colour on the palette and then, with new knowledge, comes multiple new colours that we can now utilise to shape and design our lives. All sorts of new possibilities open up in a quick manner with frequent reading and learning.

From my ignorance of not reading or learning to becoming a reader of books, I soon moved from the first phase of awareness to the next stage of understanding, and then a solid foundation from my reading, mixed with real-life experiences, which is a whole new animal. It's a process that will be life changing, no matter where you are in life, when moving from awareness to understanding.

I read travel books, history, finance, investment, military, novels, classics, biographies, personal development, sports, leadership, music and anything that I found interesting or stimulating. Benjamin Franklin said, "An investment in knowledge pays the best interest." The rewards have been phenomenal, from becoming more valuable, learning finance, investment and entrepreneurship, becoming a much better reader and applying this to life, travelling the world after becoming inspired reading about many places in travel books, understanding history and seeing it repeat itself, learning about famous military battles and the lessons involved, how to lead and communicate, and so much more, just from books.

The consequences of not being a reader were a disaster, and I can vouch for this first-hand from those experiences in my early twenties. Reading stimulates and educates, it gives us energy and new desires, makes the impossible seem possible, and provides a light from the darkness back to the light. It's also just really pleasurable to read a great book — often you don't want it to end.

There's a reason why so many greats from the past have called books their best friends.

Reading or any other form of learning, such as podcasts, CDs, and mentorship are key laws and foundations to any self-fulfilling and prosperous life.

Become a reader and never stop learning! It's the best investment you can ever make for yourself.

Set your navigation system

What are your philosophy and beliefs on anything?

Ignorance is not bliss
- Jim Rohn

The road can take you to many places

Your philosophy is your signpost in life

Frequent reading, gathering information, real-life experiences, observation and conversations with others all help develop our internal navigation system that steers and directs our lives.

Our internal navigation system is nothing more than our philosophy of life and what we believe, think and feel about certain matters.

Our philosophy is our guidance system and can be compared with which highway we will drive down throughout life. It's our road and path, our guidepost to life itself.

Developing and maintaining our navigation system is one of the core foundations to our lives, and if we do not take the time to understand ourselves, as well as our inner thoughts and beliefs, so that we can gather the right information, we can fall victim to conformity, fear, ignorance, ego, peer pressure, the media and other negative influences which will hurt us and the path we choose and decisions we make for life.

As an example, take two different philosophies with money and investing. One person believes in spending everything while another believes in saving and investing first, then spending afterwards: two different philosophies that have two totally different outcomes.

It's the same with our health. One person does not exercise, eats too much junk food and lies idle, while another exercises, gets good sleep, fasts intermittently and believes that food should be in moderation. The end result between the pair is miles apart as regards to their health, and this all starts from their philosophy.

We need to develop philosophies for money, health, relationships, politics, lifestyle, business, learning, leadership, helping others, and developing virtue and character traits, otherwise we will fall victim to negative influences in the world around us.

Your navigation system is your guidance system to life and can lead down many different roads, either by predetermined decision or default.

Take some time to really get to know yourself and the world around you through reading, personal experiences and the positive influence of others, so as not to fall victim to the world and all the bad influences.

Attitude, the magic word

*A good attitude turns the lights on
and music up in our lives*
- Earl Nightingale

Your past does not control you unless you permit it to
- William E Bailey

Nothing is good or bad but thinking makes it so
- Shakespeare (Hamlet, Act II, Scene 2)

Earl Nightingale called attitude the magic word, and there is a good reason why. Our attitudes, if we take the time to think about it, control our environment, actions and our entire view of the world. With a good attitude, anything is possible; with a bad attitude, it's hard to get out of bed.

The quickest way to know if we have a good or bad attitude is to ask right at this very moment if the world is treating us well.

If we say yes, that it is, that's a good sign that we have a good attitude to life. If we say no, that is a signal that we have a bad attitude. Anything in between signals we have a so-so attitude to life.

Many of us have bad attitudes about the past, but there is very little we can do about the past. However, there is plenty we can do about the present and future.

Bad attitudes have cost people relationships, fortunes, jobs, sales, and promotions, whilst good attitudes create endless opportunities and serendipitous moments.

Developing a good attitude is not the easiest thing to do but is something we must work on. Listen to how you think and feel, forgive yourself, let go of the past, get to know yourself better as regards what turns you on and off, and what is positive and negative in your life, including the people you associate with.

A good attitude can turn on the lights in our lives. It can turn the music up in our lives. The promise of the future is an awesome force, and we need to borrow from the future to push us forward. Our attitude depends greatly on how we see the future and the world around us, and we must design a future that excites us.

Developing a great attitude is worth more than any amount of money in the bank and is one of life's best skills we can each develop within our character. One only has to see those folks who have been dealt a bad hand such as a serious disability or major health issue, through no fault of their own, and despite such adversity and hardship, they can still carry a great attitude, often far better than those not affected by any hardship at all. They can still see the positive side of life despite such great adversity and still thrive in such circumstances. This all stems from having a great attitude, no matter what happens in life. I strongly believe having a great attitude is one of the keys to how those who face great adversity not only survive but thrive in any situation. We should follow their example.

Attitude, the magic word

Having the right attitude is often the difference between success and failure, and it all starts with how we think and feel and how we see the present and future. Earl Nightingale was spot on: attitude really is the magic word, no matter if your life is good or bad or what cards you have been dealt. A great attitude can bring magic into your life, no matter what you face.

We become what we think about

We become what we think about
- Earl Nightingale

You can't change the past but you can change the future

As a man thinketh, so he is
- Proverbs 23:7

Earl Nightingale said the six strangest words were: "We become what we think about." Such simplicity in an age of complexity and confusion! Nightingale had found the secret, like many other great thinkers who had come before him, from the Bible, Napoleon Hill, William James, Shakespeare, and Ralph Waldo Emerson, that our thoughts determine what we attract into our life and what we become. The great philosophers, prophets and thinkers have argued about many different matters throughout history, but they are in complete harmony on this one subject.

The more you think about it, the more you realise the truth in Nightingale's statement.

Drunks think about booze, drug addicts think about drugs, greedy people think about money, doctor students think about medicine, writers think about writing, girls often think about marriage and kids, golfers think about golf, and travellers think about travelling to new locations.

The truth of Nightingale's statement really struck me once whilst travelling overseas and in a time of reflection. I had reached two goals in rapid succession. The goals were a financial savings number which had taken over a decade to hit, and visiting two new countries which I had long wanted to visit. I had long thought about both goals, and in a moment of reflection, after achieving both goals, realised that I had indeed become and achieved what I had thought about, and that other goals that I thought about could also be achieved and were more than just a possibility.

On the opposite side of the coin, I had also realised the things that I had not achieved or wanted in my life. I was quite pessimistic or lacked belief, which impacted my activity and persistence to achieve those goals.

I learned that I can determine what I think about, therefore I can determine what I wish to become. That was the big lesson I learned from that day in reflection. My thinking was the great power that would take me wherever I wished to go, and only I alone could decide on what I thought about.

Winning the battle of the mind is one of the greatest challenges we all face. With so much negativity today from people, our culture, the mass media and social media, it feels like we are fighting endless negative news and pessimistic people.

The mind is an incredibly powerful instrument that we get virtually no training on throughout life, as we look on in wonder at new technology and modern creations and yet don't realise we each have the most powerful tool available in the human mind available to each of us.

Controlling our thoughts is the key to taking charge of our lives. Our thinking has led us to where we are and what we have today, and it will also lead us to where we want to be and what we want and attract in one, five, ten and twenty years' time.

We really do become what we think about, and that is the strangest secret. The mind is like a magnet and can attract both good and bad, but it all depends on what we think about.

Every failure or adversity carries a seed of equivalent advantage

This too shall pass
- mediaeval Persian Sufi poets

Maybe it was a gift

What doesn't kill you makes you stronger
- Friedrich Nietzche

The grandfather of personal development, Napoleon Hill, was one of the first modern thinkers and writers to discuss the benefits of adversity and failure.

Many, including myself, used to think failure was the end of the world and we have nothing to be proud of regarding such events in our lives.

Hill took the exact opposite view: that if we didn't let failure or adversity destroy us, there was the seed of equivalent advantage waiting to be found. It really is one of the great laws to ponder when adversity or failure strikes.

All of us will face great adversity or hardship in our lives, and often we feel overwhelmed and feel like quitting, but if we keep our heads and keep our spirits up, we can rise up from any failure and use the lessons to our benefit. Many today believe failure of any endeavour is the end of the road, but nothing could be further from the truth. The greater lessons and experiences often come from great adversity.

While adversity and failure are hard pills to swallow, which never get easier, no matter what anyone says, the benefits can be enormous. When we look back on our life, we see the stepping stones and roadblocks often were meant to lead to greater success and build greater character within ourselves, and Nietzche's quote that what does not kill you makes you stronger is worth pondering.

The failures have been often and many in my life, from redundancies, towns I have hated to live in, business and private failures, financial hardship, health issues and relationship problems, but often a greater good can come from the pain and adversity in each situation.

Jobs and businesses that I hated to work in were signals that I needed to change jobs or career, towns I didn't fit into were signals I was in the wrong place, toxic relationships were warnings that I had the wrong people in my life, who were draining my energy like emotional vampires. Being broke is one of the best ways to learn you are on the wrong path, though I suggest you don't stay too long on that path.

It is sometimes impossible to get on the right road without ending up on the sidewalk of life.

Rather than feeling overwhelmed by failure and adversity, take the higher road and look for the seed of equivalent advantage,

Every failure or adversity carries a seed of equivalent advantage

which carries wisdom, knowledge, awareness, understanding, and real experience, which is worth more than money, gold or silver and can be the key to opening the lock in due time.

You either win or learn, and that needs to be our mindset: to not let the failures tear us to pieces as we try and fail and then try and fail again and again. Failure is our best teacher. Adversity introduces a person to himself. That's when we really get to know ourselves.

Don't let disappointment, failure and adversity destroy you. If we stay persistent, there really is the seed of equivalent advantage to any adversity or failure, which will make us even greater and stronger as people, as we grow and learn and become a greater being in the world.

Rediscovery of practice

Practice makes perfect

Repetition is the mother of skills

When you first drove your car on the highway that was buzzing with cars at high speed, you were probably nervous and entered the highway with extreme caution, but now, after years of experience, you just enter with no fear and no worry about high speeds and cars whizzing by. This is the result of rediscovery of practice, which is another term for repetition or doing something over and over again.

All craftsmen become highly skillful only after years of practice at honing their skills and developing their craft. You see this with woodworkers, tradesmen, sportsmen, writers, navigators, pilots, painters, musicians, and nearly any other field, to acquire competence and mastery.

To become good at something that eventually leads to mastery, you must practise over and over again, sometimes thousands of repeated times before you master this skill and it becomes autopilot-like.

Rediscovery of practice

Tom Brady throwing a pass or Michael Jordan or Larry Bird shooting a basketball looks so easy to viewers, but only after they have repeated this action over and over again, literally in the tens of thousands.

The internet age wants everything now, but real mastery takes many, many years and many hours of sweat, tears and toil, and there is no shortcut.

Honing a craft takes years of relentless dedication, and the only way you can learn anything is with repeated practice.

Rediscovery of practice goes well beyond just honing skills. It also applies to our philosophy, learning, relationships, and health, and is closely associated with good habits and discipline.

You don't just read a book once to help you live better and become wiser; you must go over and over that book to really get it to sink in, with conscious competence from the work done that it is deep in your subconscious.

Emerson said it best: "Do the thing and you shall have the power." By doing something repeatedly and learning the results of rediscovery of practice, you will hone your craft and then have the power of competence and true mastery.

Don't watch what people say, watch what they do

Deeds not words
- George Washington

What you do speaks so loudly I cannot hear what you are saying
- Ralph Waldo Emerson

The reality factor!

Action talks, rhetoric walks
- Doc Love

Bottom-line her actions (it saves time)
- Doc Love

Show me
- Motto of State of Missouri

Never watch what people say or promise, only pay close attention to what people do in deeds!

The bottom-line factor says actions and deeds are all that matter, not what people say or promise, and is the only barometer we should measure against.

Bottom-line people's actions and you will save yourself a lot of time, disappointment and heartache.

Too often, we believe the promises people give us, from work colleagues, business dealings, political candidates, to the romantic dating game, and often this only causes great frustration and disappointment in our lives.

Throughout life, this vital skill is needed to navigate, negotiate, close a deal, form partnerships built on trust, recruit individuals who will support you in your cause or goal, and decide on who to support, such as political parties and other groups. One of life's biggest decisions for anyone is finding a romantic partner who has genuine interest in you and is not a time waster.

Time wasters are everywhere, from potential business clients who have no real interest in forming a partnership or becoming a client, potential job applicants who have no real interest in joining your organisation, to political candidates who promise the world but then do the exact opposite in deeds. One of the biggest frustrations for many is dating, as potential partners will waste your time and energy when they have no real interest in you, until someone else comes along.

Bottom line: people's actions are the best guide to their real intentions and gauging their interest level, no matter what they say or promise.

Become a person of value, not importance

Success is not to be pursued, success is attracted by what you become
- Jim Rohn

What you have is what you have attracted
- Jim Rohn

Skills pay the bills

We now live in a world where everyone seems to want fame, fortune and attention, and, with the creation and advancement of modern technology where the world is at our fingertips, we now have a world of wannabe stars, who, to be brutally honest, add very little value to the world except seeking attention.

Sadly, it is not just teens and young adults who clamour for attention on apps and social media; this is now seen across all age groups and genders around the world. They all share the need or desire to want to be noticed and have status!

Take a stroll on any Facebook, Instagram, YouTube, TikTok or X feed, and you will find tens of millions of folks every day who are looking for attention and wanting to be a person of importance, even if that means betraying their inner truth and performing ridiculous antics and stunts to gain attention and likes. They all share one thing in common, and that is the desire for attention and to be perceived as a person of importance. Status has become like a drug in a world of followers, who often lack any real meaning or purpose in their lives. Social media followers and like numbers on any post have become the modern measurement for success, while real skills and values have been lost in a world that has been turned upside-down, where the ridiculous get applauded and the great and honourable often go unnoticed.

While the definition of success today has changed for the worse, we should buck the trend and focus on becoming a person of high value and integrity first, rather than a person of importance or status.

A person of value can support their family, workplace, community and home country, and often we only realise how important they are when a time of crisis arrives.

Value can be achieved in many ways by becoming a person of integrity and honesty, who may fall, but continues to strive towards their higher ideals and standards. The development of ourselves can come from reading and studying books to become more knowledgeable; exercising and eating a good diet to become fitter, healthier and stronger, allowing us to live a life of vigour, vitality and energy; learning the disciplines and habits required; becoming a great communicator and listener, with excellent time management skills; service focused; developing our leadership capabilities to lead ourselves and others; and learning a range of skills of all types, from various trades, mentoring youth, medicine, accounting, legal, music, art, negotiation, sales, economics, history, psychology, or philosophy that suits your sweet spot and adds value to others.

Skills pay the bills, and the development of skills will make you a person of great value and help all those around you who may call on you for support.

In the Bible, Isaiah said God's hand was not short. Let that be the same for us: let us be people of great value who are wise, healthy, knowledgeable, well read and well travelled, with a diverse range of skills, who can add great value to those around us and have the answers and capabilities for any problem when difficulties or emergencies arise. This is one of the reasons why the Greatest Generation is so admired after the difficulties of the Great Depression and World War Two, as they sacrificed for the greater good and cause.

When we ourselves grow and become more valuable, our self esteem skyrockets as we grow and grow into people who move away from the limelight but are focused on adding real value and service to those around us.

Forget being a person of importance and seeking status through social media likes, and instead seek real values, character traits and skills that grow ourselves and help others. This is where true value lies.

We have everything we need

You have everything already to live an incredible life

*The best things in life come for free and
you don't even realise their power*

*What a piece of work is a man!
how noble in reason,
how infinite in faculty*
- Shakespeare (Hamlet, Act 2, Scene 2)

We often forget that everything we think we need we already have. Too often, we look at things and situations and say it costs too much, I don't have the capabilities or beliefs, not enough money, I need to know the right people, or a million other reasons and excuses as to why we can't succeed or live the life we want.

We need constant reminding that everything we need to succeed, we already have from birth, and it doesn't cost a cent. The capabilities and faculties of a human being really are incredible, and we should take some time to pause to think about what great power we all have within.

Our minds, bodies, spirits, hearts, intellects, willpower, imagination, dreams, decision-making capabilities, and thinking apparatus all come at birth for free and they are worth far more than possessions such as money, houses, cars and other things we put way more emphasis on.

Within each of us is unlimited potential, and the things we were born with and that come for free are at our disposal for any journey or challenge. We need reminding often about the great powers within each of us that too often lie dormant.

We have everything we need and we should never forget this. We are greater than any problem or adversity. The best things come for free.

Our higher mental faculties

Live mentally from the inside, rather than the outside

*Our higher faculties are where the
real genius lies within all of us*

Leave your senses out of it
- Bob Proctor

Most of our education comes from the traditional learning formats such as hearing, seeing, smelling, tasting and touching. These are the outside faculties that control our world and how we see life.

They are all essential, but our real genius comes from the inside, or, as Bob Proctor calls them, our higher mental faculties. Proctor said all humans were born and gifted with the higher faculties of intuition, perception, will, memory, reason and imagination, and the use of these faculties is where the real genius lies within each of us.

I would say most humans are not even aware of the power of our inner faculties or have received any training about them, when they come to us free from birth and hold so much power and potential.

Intuition is listening to your gut. How often has our gut warned us about a situation or person and proven to be dead right despite no facts or evidence? Intuition is an incredible instrument in helping us live better, make decisions and keep us away from the negative.

Perception is one of the greatest tools at our disposal, and it is nothing more than how we see the world, events and the future. One person sees an old vacant block of land and another sees a wave of apartments. That is the power of perception, and with so much negativity and pessimism around today, we need to tap into its power to help us see a bright and sunny future.

"Will" is another word for total focus and completely removing distractions and being focused on what we are doing in any endeavour. The will is one of the strongest mental faculties at our disposal, so strong that von Braun told President Kennedy it was the one thing required to put a man on the moon.

Despite what we have been told, our subconscious memory remembers everything, and this power can recall anything — from major life experiences to the obscure.

Reason is our ability to think and what makes us different from all the animals in the world. Our ability to reason and think has caused incredible creations and achievements and solved all sorts of problems, and it all starts with the ability to reason and think about anything.

Einstein said imagination was more powerful than knowledge, and history has proven how the imagination can design and create anything. The dreams or imagination of people is not merely daydreaming and has incredible power, despite what many think. We should cherish the power of our imagination.

Our higher mental faculties

While we may not be aware of the power of these inner faculties, bring them out and use them. They were designed to help you navigate life, and the use of these will take you to new levels you never thought possible.

Create and produce

Are you a giver or a taker?

You have to sow to reap

*Work, consume, debt, work, rinse, repeat
the life of despair and destruction*

Consumerism is one of the biggest addictions in the world today, as people rack up all kinds of debilitating debts that chain many to a life of poverty and despair, as the endless cycle of work, consumerism, debt and required work destroys our soul and spirit in the process. The push to sell anything is never-ending, with every small or major company in the world now jamming products, events and services in our face 24/7, with relentless marketing across many platforms, urging us to buy or believe that we are missing out. Our families and friends show off new cars and houses, and parade on social media with every new item, but often they are chained to ever-growing debt, and appearance can come at a great cost.

Whilst sinking in consumption and debt, we don't often ask the question: What value am I bringing to the market and am I a producer or a consumer?

Create and produce

It is a simple question we must ask and one that will quickly determine our chances for achieving financial independence and other rewards in life.

The producer and the consumer are two different roads that have completely different endings and locations, but sadly, many don't know the difference.

Whilst working in any job is noble, the laws of leverage and mathematics go against us when trying to gain a greater return, as we can only produce for the hours we are performing any duty, and thus, our leverage is very limited, as we each only have so many hours and so much energy every new day.

The consumer roadmap is the wrong road, if we are to live a greater life. Only by becoming a creator and producer can we go to the higher realms and get the better returns in life.

Sadly, the majority of the world are consumers and are chained to the death cycle of debt, consumerism and work, which is rinsed and repeated each year as the hole gets bigger and deeper.

If we are to go against the crowd and modern marketing, we must become a producer and creator. Our rewards in life will always be in exact return to our services rendered, and the only way we can receive more is to give more, to create, build and produce more, and that means becoming a producer and creator, both with our hands and minds, and through diligent activity.

The producers and creators are the few who enjoy great satisfaction with the work they perform. They get the bigger rewards and returns in life for serving more people. They turn nothing into something from a basic idea; they create businesses, products and services; make art, music and literature; manufacture and provide agricultural goods. They try to meet the needs of others while forgetting about themselves in the process; they look to use leverage and mathematics to serve more, and thus achieve a greater outcome and return.

Until we are awoken to the fact, we don't realise we have produced or created very little. Our rewards are a reflection of this. We need to take stock of our talents, interests and abilities, and see what we can do with what we have been given.

The story of the talents in the Bible is one of the greatest parables ever told: that we either use or lose what we have been given, and, if we want a return, we must get busy and produce, or at least do something.

Let's become producers and creators. Each of us can build or create something of great value that will benefit both us and the world. The satisfaction that you will feel is one of the sweetest feelings one can receive from life. The other rewards are the cherry on the cake.

Know the truth

Know the truth and the truth will set you free
- Bible (John 8:32)

The truth is incontrovertible. Malice may attack it, ignorance may deride it, but in the end, there it is
- Winston Churchill

The Good Book says: "Know the truth and the truth will set you free" (John 8:32). We live in an age of overstimulation, with an excess of information that attacks us relentlessly every day, often with misinformation, set agendas and lies from our governments and major corporations, who have put self interest before the people's best interests. Never have we needed the truth to be our guide and protect us from those evil influences more than we do today.

Without the truth, we cannot live our best life, and we must always seek the truth of the matter, no matter how hard it may be for us or how painful it is to face reality.

The truth must be our guiding philosophy to avoid danger and pain, and, as the Bible says, to set us free.

I have had many painful experiences when I have realised I have found the truth after being misled with lies, and these have come from poor financial investments, purchases of various items, relationships, career choices, and many other things. Only by finding the truth can we steer our lives down the right path and back on track.

The truth has become taboo for many today, and speaking the truth has become criminal, like in a world that has little truth and where conformity and public pressure mislead the masses, as we see political, economic and social chaos.

The truth is an incredible thing. It frees our minds from fear and worry and lets us know we are on the right path. The truth is essential if we are to be true to ourselves and live an authentic life and not be misinformed by some people and the world around us, who will do anything to force their agenda or cause, as the masses follow blindly.

Get the facts

Facts are stubborn things
- John Adams

*The source of the truth is unimportant,
only the finding of it is important*
- William E Bailey

Business icon Harold Geneen wrote a famous book called *Managing*, and one of the greatest lessons I learned from his extensive and impressive management career across the globe was to always get the facts and not rely on rumours or information that has no truth.

Getting the facts has been one of the foundations for my business and personal life. It is one skill that will save a lot of time and heartache.

When leading teams, I would often be asked to make key decisions for the organisation, but often I would not have all the information available. Unless you have the facts, it is very hard to make a wise decision. As Geneen urged, I would always push back on staff and ask for more information and want the real facts of the matter when information was grey or insufficient. Making decisions is so much easier when you have all the facts at hand and not rumours or politics in the office that will all run their own agenda.

How many bad decisions have we seen when the decision maker did not have all the facts? Countless examples are proof of the consequences of not getting the facts.

Careers, relationships, governments and businesses have all been destroyed by bad decisions stemming from not getting the facts.

Get the facts in both your professional and personal life for any key decision along your journey, and it will save a lot of time and heartache.

The truth is an incredible thing, but we often can only get the truth from getting the real facts for any matter or problem. As John Adams learned, facts are stubborn things!

Questions

Quality questions create a quality life
- Tony Robbins

Judge a man by his questions rather than his answers
- Voltaire

One of the greatest mental tools at your disposal is to ask questions of yourself to help you navigate your way through life. Asking questions can stimulate our minds and help us explore any area of our lives and the world we live in.

Deep thinking is hard work and questions are a great tool to help us put our thoughts into plans and actions, and to understand who we are and what we want and don't want from life.

It has been said that the better questions we ask of ourselves, the better quality life we can have.

Asking questions can also be used when things seem dire and there is no hope left, which can help us prepare adequately to face the situation. When things are really bad and there seems to be no light, I will ask myself the question: What is the worst thing that could happen in this situation? Strangely, once you work back from the worst possible outcome, you become better prepared to face what you are confronted with, and, strangely, things start to improve. The stress and worry that had consumed you starts to disappear once you ask what the worst outcome could be.

We can use questions for anything, including some examples below:

What do I want?
What do I want to see and have?
Where do I want to live?
What do I need to become?
What can I do to improve my relationships?
What can I do to become healthier?
How do I become financially independent?
Where should I invest my money?
What books would I like to read?
What music would I like to explore?
Where would I like to travel in the world?
What event would I like to attend?
How do I solve this problem?
How can I produce and create more?
How can I serve more?
Is this an opinion or fact?
Does this person have a conflict of interest?
How can I make more friends?
What qualities should my potential partner have?
What is the worst thing that can happen?

Questions stimulate us and open up all sorts of possibilities in our minds. Use questions and you will find answers you never thought possible that will help you live a better, exciting and more meaningful life.

Emotions rule the world

Emotions are twenty-four times stronger than logic

Emotions are reported to be twenty-four times stronger than normal logic and reason, which is why one then quickly understands why emotions rule the world and why logic and reason fail so often.

Emotions are the deep layers of the mind and heart and have far more power than most realise, and can be for both good and bad in our lives.

Times of emotional turbulence can be seen from job losses, business failures, relationship breakdowns, financial difficulties, death, stress and anxiety, scars that fail to go away, past hurts, and regrets, plus world events such as war, famine, disease and other global matters that can really shake a person with fear and worry.

We all saw the destruction of the Great Depression when the whole world was consumed with fear and worry, which led to the worst economic crash in history and destroyed many lives in the process, as people's fear and worry became manifested.

The other side of the coin can be seen when one falls in love for the first time. One cannot sleep or think about anything else, and walks the world with high feelings, and in the early days of dating, could drive all night to see their partner. Sporting and business professionals know the feelings of joy, relief and happiness when they win big in their respective endeavours and achieve grand goals.

The bad emotions we all face and must conquer are fear, greed, envy, hate, worry, doubt, jealousy and anger. These are some of the greatest challenges, as we try to master our lives and live life on the terms we want. These negative emotions can destroy lives, friendships, marriages, and careers, and unless we get control of them, they will cause great damage.

Some of our most powerful allies are love, faith, forgiveness, patriotism, loyalty, courage, honesty, generosity, joy, happiness, discipline, and belief, which have stood the test of time and have allowed many throughout the ages to conquer enormous challenges.

Controlling our emotions is one of the greatest challenges in life. Often we get no teaching or mentorship on how to handle these, and only through time do we slowly win the battle, often after inner chaos or terrible experiences.

Become aware of the power of emotions for both good and bad. They are extremely powerful. Try to destroy or limit the bad ones and cultivate the good ones in the direction that will aid your life.

Destroy what holds you in slavery

Modern slavery has chained the world

Slavery still exists

Billions of people around the world today are still held captive to slavery. I am not talking about pre civil war era slavery or slavery in Roman times when slaves would work relentlessly for nothing and be subject to an owner. That is the image that comes to most people's minds when they think of being a slave.

In much of the world, slavery is thankfully illegal today, but most people are still enslaved, without self knowledge, awareness or understanding. We are born into this world with a blank state, but slowly, over time, we imprison ourselves.

Today, the world and its inhabitants are slaves to toxic relationships, emotions, addictions of all kinds, debt, fear, false beliefs and possessions.

We see it everywhere, for example, the woman who refuses to leave her abusive partner enslaves herself by staying in the relationship and is held captive in her own prison.

We stay in jobs we absolutely hate that kill our happiness and zest for life when we know we should quit. We see people buying million-dollar houses which they can't afford and are now slaves to debt and servants to the banks

Emotionally, we see many held captive to negative emotions such as losing one's temper and having no self control. We see jealousy and envy destroy relationships of all kinds. Emotional slavery is real, and if we can't control our emotions, our emotions will soon control us.

We see psychological slavery, with people pleasers and nice guys who put others' needs before themselves to their own detriment, which then leads to bitterness and resentment as others walk all over them.

We compare ourselves to others and their achievements, which is the fast track for unhappiness, when we are all so different and unique.

The worst kind of psychological slavery is fear! People today are fearful of anything and everything that you can imagine, from COVID, to quitting a job, dying, ageing, following their passions, taking an adventure, changes of any kind, leaving a toxic relationship, financial fears or just fear of the unknown.

Fear has enslaved more people than any prison ever has, and is so prevalent and pervasive, it's like a virus that impacts the mind. Fear is the killer of dreams and future hopes, and lives and dies in the mind. It is often only an illusion in the mind.

Relationships can bring great joy and happiness into our lives but they can also be a source of great anger, frustration and sadness. Many today are stuck in toxic relationships with partners, family, friends and co-workers. Positive people are nourishing, while negative people drain your energy and life. If you don't cut toxic people out of your life, they will destroy your life. Emotional vampires steal all your joy and happiness without many of us being aware of this.

The material slave has become all too common in the Western world in recent years, as everyone tries to keep up with the Joneses with flash homes, cars and lifestyles they can't afford and are then slaves to debt. Many stay in jobs they hate but are wage slaves to jobs and become trapped in a vicious cycle. The poor and unskilled are often wage slaves, while the wealthy and educated are trapped in a cycle of debt and desire for possessions.

Lastly, we have the addiction slave, which has exploded in the modern world, with many living lives of no meaning or purpose. We see addictions of all kinds, from gambling, food, porn, drugs, shopping, social media, alcohol, video games and many more. Addictions provide an illusion of escape and comfort to numb our pain, but slowly over time, take over our lives and destroy us from the inside.

The effects of slavery mentioned are real and devastating. Slavery causes great suffering on both the conscious and unconscious level and steals our joy and happiness. It stops us from living with real authenticity and reaching our full potential and living and designing lives we most desire.

So what is the solution to slavery? There is only one option and that is to destroy what enslaves us.

Destroy what holds you in slavery

Destruction must take place before any real change can take place.

If we don't destroy what is killing us, it will kill us!

Destroy toxic relationships, limiting beliefs, the debt trap, old habits, addictions that only bring numbness and misery, fear, envy, jealousy and other emotions and fears that hold us back.

Genuine honesty, looking inwardly, is both refreshing and good for us. It has a way of setting us free and back on the right path. Living in denial will only lead to more depression, anxiety and frustration.

Destruction is something both you and I should embrace and not be fearful of. We all must be willing to destroy paths that no longer serve or support us. Only then can we rise again.

Our futures depend on it!

Time is finite, work is infinite

Either you run the day or the day runs you
- Jim Rohn

Don't mistake movement for achievement
- Jim Rohn

Nine tenths of wisdom is the use of time
- Teddy Roosevelt

*Time energy management is the
real secret to productivity*

Understanding that time is finite and work and leisure are infinite is one of the keys to prioritising our life and getting the most out of it.

Time is the one commodity that is given in equal share to us all, both the rich and poor. No matter where we live around the world, we each get 24 hours per day to choose and do as we please.

Many waste this most important commodity and few take the time to realise that time is finite and we each only have so much given to us. For some, it is much less than others, while other matters like work are infinite in their demands and have no ending.

School or work never educated me on the wise use of time, which is probably the most precious asset at our disposal, and yet provided basic information and teaching on many other subjects that are not nearly as important.

The wise use of time and resources is nine tenths of wisdom, according to former American president Teddy Roosevelt, who squeezed every last drop out of his time on Earth, from becoming president, cleaning up crime as the Police Commissioner of New York, reading thousands of books, grand adventures to the Badlands and the Nile, fighting in the Spanish War, becoming a naturalist and many other noted achievements.

Knowing and becoming aware that time is finite is critical if we are to live our best lives. Many books have been written about time management in recent years and it has become a popular topic on many podcasts, but these books and podcasts often miss the key ingredient that time is finite and our energy levels are never static.

Three things have helped shape my philosophy in the wise use of time. One is that time is finite for all; two is knowing that time is finite, we must prioritise it to match what is most important in our lives; and three, that time energy management is needed if we want to use time to the fullest.

Prioritising our time means taking time to reflect on what is most important. Our lives have many responsibilities, but determining which should get our time is critical. Work, family, health, relaxation, community, friendships, hobbies, sport, and adventure are just a few we need to look at regarding how we distribute and allocate our time. We can't do everything, like many say, but we can prioritise and focus our time on the important things.

Energy management is one of the best secrets for the use of time. Our energy levels are never static and there will be times when we will need peak energy for important matters and tasks. We should use peak energy for peak times and lower energy for less important matters. We need to understand our bodies and minds and when we have the most energy. Are we at our peak in the morning or at night?

The nap has been utilised for thousands of years by many famous men such as Winston Churchill, John Kennedy, Napoleon Bonaparte, Aristotle, Thomas Edison, Douglas MacArthur, and Frank Lloyd Wright. These are just a few who found the secret power of a quick nap to reenergize the body and mind and then re-engage in hard work.

Knowing that time is finite is the first step to wisdom in managing our time. Then it is only natural to prioritise what is important and to decide what is not important, as we give focus to the important. The real secret is the combination of time and prioritisation of energy management to create time energy management, which will provide benefits many would never believe possible.

The Eisenhower Decision Matrix

*What is important is seldom urgent and
what is urgent is seldom important*
- Dwight Eisenhower

Do you feel like you are putting out one fire after another, you're drained of energy at the end of the working day and are making no real progress on what is important in your life, and you have no real accomplishments or results to show for all your hard work and running around?

If that is true for your life, then you are probably confusing the urgent with the important.

One man who learned to identify the difference between the urgent and important was World War Two general and former US president Dwight Einsehower (Ike).

Eisenhower, who was called on to make many important and difficult decisions throughout his long and successful career, developed the Eisenhower Decision Matrix to focus on and define what was important and what was not important, and the urgency of each decision.

The core of this decision matrix was: "What is important is seldom urgent and what is urgent is seldom important."

Too often, we tend to focus all our time and energy on the urgent and believe that what is urgent is important, when, in many situations, nothing could be further from the truth.

Eisenhower's decision matrix was popularised further in Steven Covey's now famous personal growth book, *The 7 Habits of Highly Effective People*. In this book, Covey further developed Eisenhower's matrix to help us distinguish between what's important and not important and what's urgent and not urgent. Covey's matrix is set out with the following four quadrants.

The tasks in Quadrant 1 are both important and urgent, tasks that need to be dealt with immediately, and are also related to our long-term goals and mission. They can include such matters as family emergencies, a health crisis, a tax deadline, an assignment deadline, a job interview, a car repair, a school meeting at the request of the school, and paying bills.

These are all important and urgent, but in some situations, good planning can eliminate these tasks or take the urgency out of them. Having a regular maintenance schedule can reduce risks for your car and household appliances, looking after your health can reduce future health problems, and preparing papers and tax documentation on time can stop these from becoming urgent.

Although all urgent and important tasks cannot be completely removed, we can greatly reduce them by being proactive and by spending more time in Quadrant 2.

Quadrant 2 is the not urgent but important tasks quadrant. It may not seem as important on a grand scale, but these tasks must be done on a consistent basis in order to live a great and rewarding life. It is the quadrant we should prioritise and focus our time and energy on most. These tasks can consist of exercise, reading, studying, family time, catching up with friends, date nights, practising rewarding hobbies, weekly and long-term planning, meditation, journaling, taking a class to improve skills and knowledge, service focused activities and investing and saving.

This quadrant will provide the most benefit, rewards and lasting happiness for your life and for others. So we don't waste time and energy on the unimportant, the key is to ensure we have clear goals and a definite mission for our life, to know what is really important, and to live intentionally and proactively. Most people who don't spend time in Quadrant 2 or achieve any real lasting success are guilty of not knowing what they want or what is important for their life.

Quadrant 3 has the urgent and not important tasks. These are tasks that are urgent but don't help us with our goals or mission in life and often distract us from the important matters. These can often be interruptions from others, when matters are urgent to them but not us. Tasks in this quadrant can include phone calls, family requests, emails, co-worker requests and other requests that require our time and attention. These tasks can often make us feel good and important and help others, but are often not important for our own personal goals or mission in life. The nice guy is often prone to dealing with tasks in this quadrant, with the inability to say no to requests from others, which then can lead to more requests.

Many people spend a lot of time on Q3 tasks, mistakenly thinking they're working in Q1. Q3 tasks do feel important, usually being tangible tasks that help others out, which gives you that sense of satisfaction from checking something off your list.

While it is not necessarily a bad thing to perform tasks and help others in this quadrant, along with balance in Quadrant 2, it can quickly lead to frustration, burnout and resentment of others when you realise you're not making progress on your own goals in life. Becoming aware of what is important and saying no to others are practicable steps to avoid spending too much time in this quadrant.

Quadrant 4 is the not urgent and not important tasks. This is the quadrant that can take all our time and attention and is often associated with addictive dopamine hits. These tasks do not help us with our goals or mission in life. Tasks in this quadrant can include watching TV, surfing the web, checking emails, playing video games, gambling, online shopping, watching sports, and scrolling endlessly through social media feeds such as Facebook, X, and Instagram. These activities can be helpful in short bursts, but all too often, they can take all our time and kill our future hopes and dreams.

Be more like Ike Einsenhower and spend more time on the important over the urgent and non important. Reflect and define what is important in your life so the urgent and unimportant don't take control.

The Eisenhower Decision Matrix

The Eisenhower Decision Matrix is the perfect tool to help you become more focused and define what is important and not important, which can save you a lot of wasted time, future disappointment, and wasted energy, and ensure you stay on the right path towards your goals and dreams.

By investing your time in Q2 by planning and organising disciplined activities, you can prevent and eliminate many of the crises and problems of Q1, balance the requests of Q3 with your own needs, and truly enjoy the downtime of Q4, knowing that you've earned the rest.

Time is not measured by a clock

The clock is man made, universal time is real time

*You don't have twenty more years,
you have twenty more winters*

We associate time with many things, such as managing our daily life schedule, determining our biological age and the calendar year, to state just a few major ones, but this can also be misleading when that method of time is also a man-made invention that guides our lives.

How we view time and our philosophy around it will greatly influence how we live and what sort of life we will fashion for ourselves and our families.

American William E Bailey said that time is not measured by a clock, but by the number of experiences we have and the emotional intensity associated with those experiences. This is a unique perspective on time, if you give it some serious thought.

What Bailey is saying is that people can live more years by simply having more experiences with deep emotional attachment. The worker who does the exact same job and duties for ten years, no matter how noble the work is, has really had one year's experience repeated ten times, in many cases. We see this often with people who become stale and frustrated after many years on the same job. It is easy to understand why.

Winston Churchill said that during World War Two, those four to five years of the war were like 200 years, as so much was happening on a daily basis, and that he lived multiple lifetimes during the war. When you read the stories and watch the movies from that period, it is easy to understand why Churchill said this.

Many Old Testament characters in the Bible are said to have lived to 600, 700 or 800 years. Maybe seventy years of our lives would be like 700 years of their lives because of the amount of experiences and adventures they encountered. That is universal time, not man-made time.

Looking at time differently can also be a warning as to how precious it really is and how we should use it to its max. If we go fishing, travelling or hunting only once a year, instead of saying we may have thirty more years to do this, we really only have 30 more times. That quickly wakes us up and makes us realise how precious the commodity of time really is and how short life is.

Many people get to the middle years and later years in their life with regret, disappointment and frustration, thinking that the best years have passed them by and the big goals and dreams of their youth have failed to materialise, as they think time has run out or is against them. But if we follow Bailey's philosophy and associate time with experiences and the intensity associated with each experience, we can learn like Churchill and many others have, that we can have more experiences and thus live more in those years.

I have experienced this in my own life, where in a certain season nothing much has happened and it has been very quiet, but then there have been other periods where I have packed in a decade worth of experiences in one or two years, and I look back in amazement at how much has occurred when I reflect on my life.

You may be down and out or in a season of winter of your life, but know this: We can get more out of life by having more experiences in the same period and therefore live more years in the same amount of time.

That is one of the greatest reminders and lessons any person could learn, no matter how old or young you are or what your position is.

Don't water last year's crops

*Things without all remedy should be
without regard: what's done is done*
- Shakespeare (Macbeth, Act III, Scene 2)

Let the dead bury the dead
- Bible (Luke 9:60)

*Your past does not control your
future unless you permit it to*
- William E Bailey

We live in a world with record levels of mental illness of all types, ranging from anxiety, stress, panic disorders, depression, suicidal thoughts and many other mental ailments that seem to be growing by the day.

People from all walks of life seem to be struggling more and more, and looking to the future with apprehension and pessimism, more so than in past generations.

One of the biggest reasons for such apprehension is that people keep watering last year's crops. The failures and hurts, regrets and disappointments of past years keep haunting and holding many back in the past. One can't move forward into new growth and new experiences and stay in the past at the same time. Physics says two objects cannot occupy the same position at once, and this is true for humans as well.

We see this negativity and hold of the past playing out in everyday life, from a person who loses his job which he had been at for many years and yet can never recover or move forward, a relationship breakdown where one partner unexpectedly leaves the other and finds a new life and the dumped partner falls apart with a breakdown, the weight gain for many when the ghosts of the past come back to haunt them, or the person who lives in fear of financial failure after some economic event from the past that still has a hold over them, as seen during the Great Depression and the years after, when the scars of the past remained — for many, for the rest of their lives.

If we are to live life to the fullest, we must put the past behind us and move forward with confidence about what the future may hold. George Washington said we should never look back unless it was for educational purposes, but far too often, we look back and water last year's crops, which only leads to more pain and suffering in our present and future.

Our past does not control our future unless we permit it, and that is a critical fact we must understand if we are to move forward and achieve the life we want.

What's done is done, or, as the Bible says, "Let the dead bury the dead." Watering last year's crops is total destruction for any individual and a quick journey to worry, doubt, fear and apprehension and the never-ending doom loop of pessimism and fear.

Don't water last year's crops

Don't water last year's crops. What's done is done. All we can change now is the present and future. We each have the power to mould our lives.

You're either growing or dying

A tree grows in the summer and then dies in the winter

Nothing stand still

Everything is designed to grow

Nature abhors a vacuum

Quantum mechanics says that everything in the universe is either growing or dying and nothing stands still. The proof of this is for all to see, once we become aware of this perpetual law in action. The universe continues to expand, according to astronomy; the coral reefs are getting bigger under water; grass grows in the summer and then dies in the winter; a tree is either growing or dying throughout the season of its life; and a rock is either growing or disintegrating. The growing and dying phase seems to be a universal law across nature and we should take great notice of it in our own lives.

Humans are just the same: we are either growing or dying, and the minute we stop going forward, we start going backwards very quickly.

You're either growing or dying

Learning and growing is a continual process, and when we feel we are moving forward towards our goals, projects and dreams, we feel so much better about ourselves and give off great energy and inner radiance. Growth, as in nature, is both natural and normal, and it seems we are designed or built for this by our creator.

The opposite is true: when we stop moving forward from pursuing new goals, experiences and new adventures, inwardly we start going backwards very quickly. Just like nature, the process does not happen overnight, but it nonetheless does happen. The person who gets off the diet and exercise plan gains the weight back quite quickly; the husband who starts taking his wife for granted soon ends up with a divorce; spending a little too much money each month leads to future debt and bankruptcy; not reading or learning, you will lose ground fast, fall behind your peers and won't have the answers to the challenges of your own life.

Everything in the universe is designed to grow, and humans are the same. It seems the creator who designed the universe had this as a universal law.

The past does not control our future unless we permit it to, and we can shape the future we want as long as we don't allow the past to shape our present and future. That is the same as disintegration in nature. There are many stories of people from around the world who have come from nothing and rose to incredible heights, which is nothing more than growth.

For things to get better, we must get better, and that all starts with personal growth. That process and zest for life should never end.

Everything in life is designed to grow and that includes us.

Resistance always comes

Fear is the only friction in thought
- William E Bailey

Resistance is absolutely certain to come in any endeavour that we are following that has our heart heavily invested in it.

Steven Pressfield wrote the signature book on the subject of the self titled *Resistance*. Pressfield talked about how creative types will certainly face great resistance and adversity in any endeavour of life along their journey.

I learned some harsh lessons about this when chasing many big goals or creative projects, and experienced firsthand the resistance that Pressfield talked about in his book.

Every major goal that I have chased after has always encountered heavy resistance, and most projects would end up taking two to four times longer than I expected. The resistance would come in many forms: failure, people letting me down, doubts, fears, money and cashflow problems, procrastination, lack of discipline, lack of action, wasting time on tension-relieving activities, and external parties and events which I had no control over.

Pressfield says the author faces this every day when he doesn't want to sit in the chair and do the most important habit of the day, which is sitting down at the desk and writing.

The minute we make up our mind to go after something significant, we can be assured that resistance will shortly be coming our way. It seems like we have to pass through a great trial in order to meet our objective, and that trial is heavy resistance.

It's a strange thing, but I have recognised that we don't face resistance in matters when our heart or spirit is not into a project or some other thing. I experienced this with some jobs I hated, and had a poor attitude. I never faced resistance with those roles like I did with creative and business goals and projects, where my heart was really desiring to achieve. Expect resistance if you are passionate about any endeavour that stirs your soul. It's a rite of passage we all must go through to succeed.

Feelings follow actions

Self discipline leads to self esteem

Do the thing and you shall have the power
 - Ralph Waldo Emerson

One of the best lessons I have learned is that feelings and motivation follow actions and not the other way around, as we have so often been told by many supposed experts.

They say to do good we must feel and think good, but this is totally false.

Many times I don't feel like exercising, writing material, playing music, reading, mowing the lawn, cleaning, or doing other forms of mental and physical work, and this can often lead to procrastination and idleness, which erodes our psyche and self esteem.

The solution I found is to just get started with any action, no matter how small: a small walk around the block, just putting your sneakers on, writing the first sentence of your book, reading just one page of a new book, starting to play your guitar or other instrument, sketching your painting, starting the mower, making your bed, washing the first dish or anything you need to do.

What you will find is that within a short amount of time, you will just feel better, and what was really hard is a mental barrier. All the motivation and talk can never swap for doing the work. That is where the real power lies. If you just start, you will soon complete what you set out to do but without relying on feelings and motivation.

If you just start, soon you will be in a nice groove and rhythm, and what seemed so hard to get going is well behind you. You now have momentum and are building discipline and the great pride and feelings of accomplishment that will follow the work you complete.

Just start and do the work and the great feelings and motivation will soon follow.

Emerson was right — do the thing and you shall have the power!

Calmness

The strong, calm man is always loved and revered. He is like a shade-giving tree in a thirsty land, or a sheltering rock in a storm
- James Allen

Calmness is power

Calmness of mind is one of the beautiful jewels of wisdom
- James Allen

Calmness is the motto I try to live by every day and is probably my favourite word in the English language. The word just exudes serenity and peace, both internally and externally.

Obtaining the state of calmness is one we should all aspire to reach and yet is a very hard state to obtain, with emotions often overriding logic and reason.

The amygdala in the brain can override logic and reason and cause rash responses to emotional and sensitive situations, and we often question our response.

The calm strong person has become extremely rare in the modern internet age, with distractions of all kinds destroying that dependable presence of the one who stands strong and calm despite the heavy winds blowing from all directions. Today, people are more stressed, angry, bitter, resentful, fearful and emotional than ever before — the exact opposite to calmness. The ugly culture we see in the West is designed to divide and conquer, outrage, cause conflict, and create sensation and tension, and yet millions flock to watch this trash across media and independent outlets, with many making huge profits off such toxicity in human nature.

How often have we seen a person ruin or sour their lives with an explosive temper and have little self control?

James Allen, in his wonderful short book *As a Man Thinketh*, finishes with a chapter on serenity, which discusses the calm person in detail. While most of the book is about controlling our thoughts to create the life and world we want, it is no surprise that he ends the book discussing calmness. Isn't the person who controls their thoughts also a calm and serene person? You can't be calm if you can't control your thoughts. The mind is the steering mechanism in our response to any situation, both positive and negative, and the cultivating of calmness puts us in complete control.

Self control is strength, thought is mastery, and calmness is power, as Allen says.

Focus on contribution and service first

Our rewards in life will always be in direct proportion to our contribution
- Earl Nightingale

You must sow to reap

Earl Nightingale said your rewards in life will always be in exact proportion to your service. The more we serve and contribute, the more we can expect to receive. It's basic mathematics, and, just like the law of cause and effect, it is a universal law that governs the world.

Sadly, I was never taught this in school or in any workplace. The focus of many of those organisations and institutions was on getting a well-paid job, which is noble but is very limited with leverage when working a 40-hour week or trying to get as much money from the customer or client as possible, even before trying to build any long-term relationship. It was an attitude of take, not service first.

Greed has become an all too common occurrence around the world, as the majority look to take before sowing. It is seen from cab drivers scamming international customers with outrageous fees, major airlines raping customers with excessive prices on many routes, or big chains and banks that make record profits off the people, and the growing monopoly of the ultra-rich class across many sectors.

It's not just the big end of town who are greedy; many of the poor and lazy are also as guilty in their own way of being selfish, often looking for handouts from the government and content to stay in this position for years without making any real attempt to roll up their sleeves and do some hard work, as the diminishing taxpayers cop the bill.

We can always quickly examine our service and contribution and look at what we are receiving in the way of money and rewards. If we are not happy with the money or the things we have acquired, we only have to look at amending our contribution and service for this to all change.

While a job is noble, it is limited in its ability to serve more people, to serve the greater masses and reach more people. We need to look at what we can build, produce and create with our entrepreneurial skills to get a far greater return.

The man says to the wood-burning stove, "Give me heat and then I will give you wood." It does not work that way. We must put the wood in first if we want a return. Contribution and service are our path to recognition and rewards of all types.

There is no luck, only causes

The law of cause and effect is the law of laws
- Ralph Waldo Emerson

Shallow men believe in luck. Strong men believe in cause and effect
- Ralph Waldo Emerson

You are the only variable
- William E Bailey

Why are some people lucky and others not lucky? Ralph Waldo Emerson said the law of cause and effect was the law of laws. Everything in the universe operates on the law of cause and effect, and our world is no different.

Everything happens because of causes and that is why we have effects for both good and bad.

If I drop something heavy on my toe and injure myself, that is not bad luck — that is a result of a cause that resulted in the effect and injury. It's a natural law and not random luck, as so many today think.

Is the person who eats well, exercises, gets good sleep just lucky for being fit and healthy or is it the input's creating healthy effects?

Is the person who invests in Bitcoin at $1k and now has become rich with the price at $100k just lucky or is this a result of cause and effect?

Most people think they are unlucky and make things far worse for themselves with a negative attitude and outlook on life and believe success and happiness only come to the lucky, rich or more fortunate.

All the mistakes and failures in my life were not a result of luck but were the result of negative causes from me losing control of my emotions, spending too much money, accepting jobs that I was not suited for, not doing enough due diligence on important matters, not being aware of many opportunities and missing out, and much more.

Sure, bad things and events do come into our lives at times and it's often no fault of our own that we have no control over them, but we can take the steering wheel of our lives and do what we can.

Good things that happen to us or come to people are a result of healthy thinking and strong actions, not as a result of random luck or chance, and we should remember this and know we can do a lot to improve our lives and not take the mystic outlook.

There has to be a cause for what we have attracted in life, and, nine times out of ten, the problem is our thinking and actions for both good and bad. Each of us determines and builds our own world through thoughts and deeds.

As Emerson said, cause and effect is the law of laws and we should never forget this, as it will determine what we receive in life both good and bad. There is no luck about what we get.

Knowledge is experience

The only source of knowledge is experience
- Albert Einstein

I do not wish to hear about the moon from someone who has not been there
- Mark Twain

In the business world, everyone is paid in two coins: cash and experience. Take the experience first; the cash will come later
- Harold Geneen

What do you know most? How about what you have experienced in life? Most people pause and struggle when asked that question and never give any real thought to what they really know or understand about themselves or life. The definition of an education or knowledge has become very misunderstood in an age of complexity, with modern curriculums that are dumbing people down. Critical thinking is becoming more and more rare.

Albert Einstein knew this and famously stated, "Learning is experience. Everything else is just information" — such simplistic wisdom in an age of confusion and mass information.

Knowledge is experience

Each of us at this very point is the sum total of our thoughts, decisions, and experiences.

Information and awareness are wonderful, and open up all sorts of possibilities for our lives, but they are also just the beginning and not the end of the process.

The end of the process is actual experience, and the combination of experience and awareness is when we really gain knowledge and wisdom.

Real knowledge based on actual experience is everywhere in our daily lives, but it is worth reminding ourselves of this. The mother who finds a new recipe in a cooking magazine now has awareness of a new dish, but this is not the same as the same mother who in twelve months' time has cooked the new recipe twenty times and knows it without needing a recipe. It's one thing to become aware of a new recipe but a totally different animal with actual experience, and that is what real knowledge is. That mother now knows that recipe back to front, after extensive experience of cooking the dish, and can stand on the concrete of truth about this recipe with actual experience, which is far deeper than just awareness or information.

The mother who has gone through her first pregnancy is much more prepared, knowledgeable and calm for the second or third birth. She now knows what her body will do, what to expect, how the hospital staff will perform, what the environment will be like and what she must do to prepare for the new birth. The doubts and fears of the first pregnancy have now been replaced by actual experience and real knowledge.

To be a master of any skill requires real experience, be it trades, teaching, writing, sport, investing, parenting or any other field you could possibly imagine.

We live in a world that is moving away from Einstein's definition of knowledge and is drowning in information overload, with podcasts dominating streaming platforms and the internet, and reading endless books but not going to the next step and gaining actual experience.

Information and awareness are wonderful, but experience is knowledge, and we should never forget this important truth. Only by gaining real experience can we gain both knowledge and mastery.

Environment is more important than heredity

Environment is but his looking-glass
- James Allen

Your living and working environment is another subject that gets very little discussion or thought but is critical to both happiness and success in one's life.

If you find yourself in the wrong environment, it will be an anchor on your ship of progress, whilst the right environment can only support your happiness, productivity and joy.

I have learned that the environment is more important than heredity factors!

We see this with people stuck in poor relationships, jobs with staff members that are a negative influence, students stuck in class with misbehaving students, and any living environment that creates friction and tension.

I learned this the hard way, with many bad decisions to join workplaces that were not the right cultural fit for me, and in my younger days of house sharing, living with people I did not know, who created a nightmare environment and only caused arguments and fights.

It is impossible to move forward in life if the environment is negative. Without a sound foundation that supports you, you are in for a world of pain. I learned this first hand.

Charlie Tremendous Jones has one of the greatest quotes ever, that "You'll be the same person in five years except for the people you meet and the books you read."

The environment and people we associate with can either be negative or positive, but the consequences of a negative environment are harsh. I have learned the hard way to always be very careful of what environments you join and who you associate and spend time with.

Cultivate the environment that will support and boost your life and not one that will create drama and friction and hold you back.

The only security comes from within

God helps those who help themselves
- Old Baptist quote

No one is coming to save or rescue you

The highest form of maturity any person can have with his or her life is to take full responsibility for the results, both the good or bad. No matter what has happened and will happen, we must take full responsibility and take charge of our lives. Sadly, more and more people are now looking to the government and others to provide support and security for them, and, in the process, are losing the highest form of maturity we can each find in responsibility.

I have learned there is no security in the many things we have been told about. There is no longer security in jobs, with many people finding this out the hard way. The old days of a job for life are long gone today, with globalisation, technology, AI, greed, industrial laws and many other things destroying what was common thought in the industrial era.

Many now look to the government to provide for them, as we witness the expansion of government impacting our lives, which grows more and more, and we feel it more, with higher inflation and taxes as the government gets bigger and bigger and the costs to maintain this rise for the everyday Joe.

The only real form of security comes from within, and that is developing the graces, knowledge, attitude, thoughts, characteristics, and skills that don't care which way the wind blows. They trust themselves from within and know they can set a good sail no matter which way the wind blows, and overcome any challenge or adversity.

The only real form of security comes from within, and it is up to each of us to find it and develop it.

Riches come in two forms

Wealth is paid in two forms: tangible and psychic

When we think about wealth and riches, the default thinking of our minds is usually about how much money we can earn or what possessions we can purchase, such as a home, a car and other nice things.

The thinking that riches and money come in only one form is wrong, as there is another form of riches that is often overlooked or not discussed and is probably more important.

Earl Nightingale was the first person I ever heard speak on this matter with such clarity and wisdom. Nightingale said riches come in two forms: the tangible form is the material form of wealth such as money and possessions, but the other form that is often forgotten is psychic wealth: the satisfaction you get from doing your job or function well and one you enjoy performing to high standards.

Most of modern culture and education today is focused on the material side of riches, but if we don't gain psychic wealth, all our endeavours will be in vain. Just earning money and having no satisfaction from the work you perform is not success or happiness.

You see these trappings everywhere, from the lawyer who hates law, the accountant who hates spreadsheets, a doctor who studied medicine only because his family were all doctors, or a tradie who follows his parents into the field when he has no interest whatsoever and would rather be in other work that stirs his spirit.

I spoke about this earlier, how in my own life, I had left school and hated the job I was performing, and had also disliked another professional job in my late twenties.

The weight that comes off our shoulders when we find work that is both interesting and stimulating cannot be underestimated. Work that we enjoy turns on the lights in our lives with a better attitude and a sincere desire to perform the work at a higher quality. The energy vibrations we give off both within and to the people around us are very noticeable to all.

Time drags when we hate the work we are doing, but it is the complete opposite when we are doing work we enjoy. That is why both forms of riches are critical to our success and happiness.

The joy we experience from doing a job well or achieving a big goal is often a far greater reward than the actual money we receive; often the money is a bonus on top of our labour. No amount of money can buy the psychic wealth we receive from work we really enjoy and are good at.

Riches come in two forms

Real wealth comes in two forms: material wealth and psychic wealth, and each is necessary if we are to be stimulated, happy and content in life.

Money is just a magnifying glass

Money will only make you more of what you already are
- William E Bailey

You learn a lot about people from money. You see the best and worst in people, and it often tells you the deeper workings of any individual and where their true values lie.

The biggest lesson I have observed about people with or without money is that money is a magnifying glass; it simply makes you more of what you are!

The proof is everywhere for our own eyes and through experiences. The drunk who gains wealth just drinks a better brand and more of it, the generous person gives more money away to local charities, the consumer just buys more expensive things, the traveller visits more countries around the world, the farmer buys more land and the entrepreneur looks for new opportunities to expand.

Money really is a magnifying glass and makes us more of what we already are. We know that is true if we give it some honest thought.

Money is not bad or good, but what we do with it and what we become in the process should always be on our minds.

Money is just a magnifying glass

Money is a necessity, despite what some say, often misrepresenting the Bible quote that so many people refer to ("For the love of money is the root of all evil" - 1 Timothy 6:10), and is essential to living a good life, as it can provide freedom and allow us to help others. But it does not make us a better person — that must come from within through the building of our character, which often takes a long time and through many trials and failures, especially if we start with nothing.

Money is to be enjoyed and used wisely and can be an incredible instrument to fashion the life we could have only dreamed about, but we also must always remember that money is a magnifying glass and simply makes us more of what we really are. So it is wise to check up regularly on the things money can't buy.

Straight satisfy thyself of the truth

Straight satisfy yourself
- Shakespeare (Othello, Act I, Scene 1)

Know the truth and the truth will set you free
- Bible (John 8:32)

English playwright and writer William Shakespeare gave some of the wisest and best life advice in recorded history when he urged people to satisfy themselves as to the truth in all situations and let truth be our guide in life and all decisions.

We live in a world where conformity or following the crowd has become the norm, but just tagging along with the majority is going to lead to a world of pain if we are not careful.

I too, was once one of the conformers, often following the crowd, believing the newspapers, people and major media networks without questioning the truth, when what they were pushing in reality was often lies, incorrect assumptions, propaganda or hidden corporate agendas that mislead the people.

Adolf Hitler blinded the masses as he surged to power with relentless propaganda, or, as he said, if you tell a lie long enough, people will eventually believe it.

We live in dangerous and divided times, and the same tactics Hitler and many other leaders have utilised in the past to gain control and power are again being used today, from the COVID propaganda, incorrect inflation data, the true state of the economy, legacy media lack of real independence, geopolitical conflicts and political and social instability.

We cannot live an authentic or free life without having the truth as our guidepost in how we behave and the decisions we make in life.

Truth has to be the foundation and guide for our lives if we are to navigate it successfully and live with internal peace against the push and pull of the modern world, even if this causes pain and discomfort.

In all situations, straight satisfy yourself as to the truth of it. Look for truth in everything, and, as the Bible says, know the truth and you will be set free!

Total focus

Totality begets totality, normality begets normality

They give you two shots to putt on a par four golf hole; that should tell you something about the ability to focus and concentrate

The will is one the greatest powers available

The art of focusing is becoming harder and harder in the digital age, with distractions beyond comprehension today that past eras would've thought impossible or unfathomable. Phones, computers, internet, YouTube, television, social media, electronic games, Netflix and other streamers, Spotify music, endless news, entertainment and sports are all at the push of a button and have relentlessly intruded into our lives in the last twenty years, and, in the process, have dramatically weakened our ability to focus and concentrate on one single task.

Addiction to phones, video games, computers, social media, the internet and other inventions has become a pandemic around the world, as people allow technology to intrude on their lives.

Total focus

The creators of these products designed them so we would become addicted, needing dopamine hits, just like how drug users get hooked on drugs or gamblers get addicted to slot machines. The need for a dopamine hit is the same button for any need such as sex, porn, food, money, gambling, shopping.

The use of the will or to give something your total focus is one of the greatest powers that we have, but sadly, it lies dormant in most people. Very few learn how to direct all their energies to one specific task and block out all forms of distraction. It's an art and extremely difficult to master. Most people's ability to focus has declined in the modern world and it is something I have struggled with greatly.

Total focus is superman-like in the ability to achieve and get things done, and is often the difference between winning and losing. The team which has better focus will always beat the team which may turn off for only one minute in a game. Golf is a perfect example of a sport with the ability to focus and repeat a habit, with a par four golf hole designed to give you two putts. That should tell you enough about total focus and the ability to repeat something. It's not how far you can hit the ball, but where you hit it, and that is a great metaphor for any endeavour in life about focusing on where we want to go.

Anyone who achieves mastery in any area has also gained mastery of focus. Writers, sportsmen, tradesmen, sailors, and probably any occupation you can think of needs mastery of focus if that person is to reach the pinnacle of his or her chosen field.

When we get focused, we become like a razor-sharp knife or a laser beam.

Werner Von Braun was asked by John Kennedy what it would take to put a man on the moon. Von Bruan replied, "The will to do it!"

That should tell you something about the use of the will and giving something your total focus and what can be achieved when you do so! John Kennedy's outrageous goal to put a man on the moon was reached in less than a decade, and that was all down to total focus.

One hour a day

One hour a day can make your dreams become a reality

Work full time on your job and part time on your fortune
- Jim Rohn

A well-known author said the secret to becoming a professional writer was to write for one hour a day, six times a week. Consistently repeating that formula, you would churn out many books and other material.

Just one hour a day used wisely can totally change our lives if we give it total focus and repeat it consistently over a long period of time. What applies to the writer can apply to any field, from starting a side gig, exercising to become fit and healthy, reading to become more knowledgeable in any field, studying diverse material, learning another language, writing a novel, teaching or mentoring, training in any sport, learning how to drive, learning how to dance, starting a new hobby, spending quality time with friends and family, learning to play the piano or guitar, learning how to draw and paint, and anything we could imagine or that interest us.

Just one hour a day can totally change our lives. The amazing thing is, we can still work full time on our jobs and work part time on our hobby or side gig and create something meaningful, either for fun or potential income and personal satisfaction.

I took this advice, and both of my books have been written by using just one hour a day six times a week to create content. When we are focused and use our time well, anything can be achieved and created from nothing. Many of the greatest creations around us from music, art, and books came from just using one hour a day better to create something. Many people have transformed their health by using just one hour a day far more wisely.

What could you use just one hour a day to create, build, improve or maintain? Our minds are limitless, so give it some thought and start using just one hour a day. It may change your life forever.

Fear is your greatest enemy

The only friction in thought is fear
- William E Bailey

Fear is the most destructive of all negative emotions

You were never born with fear

Upon the plains of hesitation lie the bare bones of those who failed to go forward at the moment of victory
- William E Bailey

There are many enemies you will face in the game of life, but one of the biggest, without doubt, is fear!

Throughout the ages, much has been written and said about fear and the deadly consequences if one is to fall victim to one of the greatest diseases of the mind that has controlled billions of people throughout history.

Fear, like many of the other lessons discussed in this book, is not taught or understood in any school curriculum or workforce that I ever participated in, which is incredible when you think of the destruction it has caused throughout history and how it has stopped so many people from living the lives they had always hoped and dreamed about.

Fear comes in many shapes and sizes, from fear of the unknown, fear of failure, fear of loss, fear of financial failure, fear of losing a job, business failure, fear of insecurity, fear of change, fear of rejection, fear of what others will say, and fear of death, and can paralyse an individual with worry and doubt.

Fear can be likened to a car running without oil. The car just seizes up. Humans, when struck by fear, are no different.

The sad thing about fear is quite often it only exists in one's mind and has been put there by the individual through past events such as failure, rejection or a traumatic event that now controls the person's present and future with fear and worry. You were never born with fear. It is a learned thing that we must remove, just like a weed in a garden.

The best antidote to our fears is to first become aware of the fear and bring it out into the sunlight of truth and see it for what it really is. Often, we see it is really nothing to be fearful of, but only to be understood, or, as so many writers have defined: false evidence appearing real.

Actually, becoming aware of what we are fearful of is a huge step in removing fear. We ponder how it got there, what it really is and how we are going to get rid of it. Nothing good comes from fear. It's like removing a weed in a garden: now we know we have it, we must pluck the roots of it out.

Caesar in Shakespeare's play Julius Caesar said, "Cowards die many times before their deaths;

The valiant never taste of death but once" (Act 2, Scene 2), as they play the event out over and over in their mind. Fear takes complete control of the mind and then the body, and the simulation becomes like it is real.

If we don't become aware of our fears and control them, they will control our lives and our actions on a daily basis. Awareness is the first step to fighting off the great emotion of fear: seeing it for what it really is and all the damage it is causing in our lives.

The next step is action and running towards your fears, the complete opposite in today's world, where people avoid fear at all costs. The fear then controls their lives, and, rather than confront these fears head on, they persist, for many, throughout their lives. People often avoid and procrastinate and allow fear to tighten its grip on their life and future, and sadly, stop them from reaching their potential.

A law of physics says that two objects cannot occupy the same position at once, and so it is with fear or faith. Both cannot be in the mind at the same time!

The only friction in thought is fear, and once it is removed, we can soar as we were designed to do, and have total clarity of mind and body. Faith is the complete opposite and we must cultivate this and other positive emotions rather than the most deadly of all emotions, fear.

Nothing good comes from fear and we must destroy it and fight it all the days we breathe.

Procrastination is the second greatest enemy

Success is nothing more than a few simple disciplines, practiced every day
- Jim Rohn

Failure is a few errors in judgement, repeated every day
- Jim Rohn

If fear is our greatest enemy, then procrastination is the second greatest threat we will face from within and the next great giant killer of creating a great life.

While fear forms inside the mind and becomes a terror of destruction in the imagination, as the mind becomes paralyzed with fear, procrastination is far more sly and subtle in its potential effects, but the end result over a lifetime is just as destructive as fear.

Procrastination is putting off what should be done today. It's the complete opposite to the discipline or good habits that we discussed earlier. Putting something off for a day or two seems just a little thing and nothing major, but if you keep doing this, over a lifetime, you will end up with major regret and disappointment about what might have been for one's life.

The path to success or failure is very slight and significant and that is why procrastination must be destroyed and replaced with discipline and good habits.

Jeff Olson in his great book *The Slight Edge* talked about how good habits repeated lead to health, wealth, friendships and a successful life, while putting off what should be done with procrastination leads to a life of misery, with poor health, money problems, broken relationships and our talents wasted.

Jim Rohn, one of Jeff Olsen's major influences, said success is nothing more than a few disciplines practised daily, while failure is a few errors in judgement, repeated every day.

A pilot for a major airline must complete a checklist before the plane is allowed to depart from an airport, and we should apply the same principle to our lives on a daily basis.

Define what you need to do on a daily basis to get the health you want, the finances you desire, to keep relationships healthy, and to be successful with the creative sources you are pursuing.

Be warned: What is easy to do is also easy not to do, Jim Rohn says. It's like eating an apple or taking a walk around the block, which are easy to do but are just as easy to not do.

Procrastination may seem harmless, but we must fight it all our lives, as it will persist until our last breath.

Don't put off what can and must be done today. The habit can be formed either way. And, as Jim Rohn said, "We must all suffer from one of two pains: the pain of discipline or the pain of regret. The difference is discipline weighs ounces while regret weighs tons."

Ego - man's Achilles heel

People learn from their failures. Seldom do they learn anything from success
- Harold Geneen

We have talked about many of the deadly emotions that are part of the mental horsemen of the mind. One that was mentioned and is worth mentioning again is ego — the male's blind spot and Achilles heel.

If I was to say the worst diseases of the mind — to go along with fear and procrastination, as discussed — I would say, in my life, ego is the other deadly emotion which has destroyed many careers, friendships, and relationships. This is when a person becomes all knowing and loses all humility.

Harold Geneen said ego was the biggest career destroyer he witnessed in his long and successful business career, and that it was far worse than alcohol, inappropriate relationships, and other career destroyers in the workplace.

I too, like Geneen, have witnessed up close the destruction of ego when someone becomes consumed with their own abilities, knowledge and power. Usually men are the worst offenders for becoming egotistical.

The egoistic person becomes all knowing, thinks he has all the answers, looks down on other staff, stops listening or consulting with their team, won't admit mistakes and thinks everyone is to serve him, and, little by little, people begin to detest this person, and the career or relationship destruction begins.

Ego is a drug and it blindsides a man to the realities around him. He comes to live in a world of his own deluded imagination, with illusions of his own making.

It seems today everyone wants recognition or to receive applause and praise, from politics, business, sporting stars, musicians, YouTube, and social media.

Ego blinds a man to his own vanity, as he loses sensitivity to the feelings and thoughts of others. He loses common sense and objectivity and becomes a menace to all in his path, especially with decision making, and he can only handle yes people.

While self confidence and power will fool some people for a while, the arrogant person will always be found out in any relationship, as their actions and antics of all knowing eventually wear thin.

People eventually detest such a person, with gossip behind their back and lack of respect growing day by day that eventually leads to a total breakdown of the relationship. He eventually can only tolerate a yes man, as the conditions deteriorate. An egotistical maniac is drunk with power.

He can't be taught, won't listen, and power goes to his head. The promising promotion, new business or relationship ends in a train wreck.

Ego is deadly in its consequences and we should all be wary of it, especially when we are receiving a promotion, success, public praise or flattery, as these things can quickly go to our heads and we lose our grip on reality and become consumed with ego.

Ego is the man's blindspot and Achilles heel. You have been warned! Humility, failures and some honest people around you should all be cultivated, as ego is one of the ugliest things you will ever see. You definitely do not want to succumb to it.

Stop doing list

Do you have a stop doing list?

If I asked you if you currently or if you have ever had in the past a to do list, there is a fair chance you would say yes. But if I asked you the same question but in reverse (flipped it): if you had a stop doing list, I would probably assume you don't have one.

Discipline, as mentioned earlier, has to be the foundation to our lives and routine, but we often forget to identify things we need to stop doing or limit to take full control of our lives.

While it's very important to have discipline and key priorities, it is just as important, and in many ways more important, to have a stop doing list. You can't have true discipline and have a multitude of bad habits at the same time.

It's hard to get great results if you mix discipline with bad habits. We see this with money, health, business and relationships, and often the things that we do too much hurt our results the most.

Stop doing list

A really bad habit or addiction can really hurt us. Our focus, awareness, energy and time is spent on bad habits, when really, we should not be doing them or they should be a low priority.

Often, if we can just limit or stop the bad habits, our lives become so much better, and the results and changes for the better occur quite fast.

Eating the wrong foods, drinking too much, associating with the wrong people, spending too much time on social media, surfing the net, not getting enough sleep, spending too much on credit cards are many activities that many people spend way too much time on and have huge ramifications to their lives.

Like nearly everyone, I have had my fair share of bad habits and have needed constant reminding of their negative impact. These have included surfing the net for hours, Netflix binge-ing, checking emails way too often, wasting money on silly items, and watching too much sport. These are not necessarily bad and can be healthy in small doses but not when they are out of balance with key priorities. A stop doing list is the cure to stay on track.

The first key to stop any bad habit is first to become aware of it and then develop a stop doing list which is written on paper and is aligned with your goals so you know what your key priorities are and what you need to stop or limit doing.

We can incorporate technology support to help us in our fight to stop or limit the bad activities and we should try and have an accountability partner with us on our journey who can hold us accountable.

We need to be reminded more than instructed, so keeping a stop doing list is always a priority to ensure you do more of the good and less of the time wasting and unhealthy activities that rob us of our futures and joy.

The wisdom to do nothing

It takes wisdom to do nothing

Nothing good comes when emotions are high

It's better to walk away and come back with a clear mind

Arguments pour fuel onto the fire

It's not needed now

One of the most uncommon forms of wisdom I have learned is, strangely, to do nothing. Often we are told to act and make decisions immediately, but in some situations, the wisest course of action is to do nothing. This is counterintuitive to most advice.

All my failures in my life were due to a rush of blood to the head, which resulted in reckless actions which I would often later regret: losing my temper and then saying or doing something foolish that would offend another person and destroy that relationship, when I would have been far better saying and doing nothing or removing myself from that environment or situation until I was in a far better state of mind to deal with the matter.

It's not easy, but sometimes the best thing you can do is to actually do nothing or remove yourself completely from the situation. This requires enormous self control and restraint from our natural emotional reactions plus the peer pressure we receive from others and the workplace, which can make it even harder. Emotions are twenty-four times stronger than logic, and can override our brain in many situations. It takes enormous self control and lots of practice to override this part of your brain when in a difficult situation.

Many psychologists recommend when making a big decision to sleep on the matter for 24-48 hours before making any decision. I have found this to be beneficial.

Doing nothing in times when this is required is not procrastination or being lazy. It can often be wise, when you take time to get a hold of your emotions, get more time to get the facts and then can come back later with a clear mind with far more understanding, self control, and wisdom.

I learned the value of doing nothing or removing myself from the environment in many situations when in leadership roles: to say or do nothing when I knew there would be no benefit gained at that time, to allow more time to get the facts to make a better decision and ensure my emotions and others were not controlling or pressuring me when emotions and tempers were high in emotional situations.

Next time you face a really sensitive situation with yourself and others or are unsure what to do and you have some time on your side, do and say nothing that you will later regret, and take some time to think it over. Let your emotions cool

The wisdom to do nothing

off before you say or do something stupid. You will find that doing nothing is a far better option than any rash or loose response, which only causes more damage and anger, and leads to regrets, reputational damage and broken relationships.

Quitting is a skill

*Contrary to popular belief, winners
quit a lot. That's how they win*
- Annie Duke

*You've got to know when to hold 'em, know when to fold
'em, know when to walk away and know when to run*
- Kenny Rogers

The old quote says: Winners don't quit and quitters don't win! I think that statement is dead wrong. While there is no doubt that persistence is required and is a necessity for the success of any endeavour, it is also necessary in life to know when to quit.

The world sees and paints quitters as having some major character flaws and that the person has weakness, but the opposite can be true. Knowing when to quit is a very valuable skill to learn.

Quitting is sometimes the difference between winning and losing, and recent studies have reported that those who quit strategically are more successful than their peers who persist and gain no positive ground for their goal or desire.

Quitting is a skill

We all will be required to quit things in our life, from relationships, personal beliefs, jobs, associates, university, bad habits, or even climbing a mountain or running a marathon when we know it is not wise to continue on.

It all really depends on context, and both persistence and knowing when to quit are essential life skills. Each situation will depend on your own personal circumstances.

We all have limited time, limited resources and limited attention that we can devote to anything at one single time, and often we will be required to decide what is most important in our lives. The art of quitting will be required to navigate life and determine what is a priority.

We have to evaluate our goals and see where we are with those goals, and if we are not making progress, whether we continue on with persistence or look to quit after a time of reflection and wise counsel.

We often feel shame with quitting a goal, when often it can be the best thing for us and allow us to recreate ourselves and realign priorities. The sunk cost fallacy is real and one that can hold us back in life when we have put in enormous effort on relationships, goals, jobs and businesses and decide to quit, but feel the weight of what has been done.

Two strategies that author Annie Duke recommends are, firstly, asking what does that mean and are there signals that this goal is warning you that you are off track and it might be best to walk away? These can be numbers, intuition, wise counsel, time spent, feelings and many other things. Think in advance what this might look like as you pursue your goal.

The second strategy is to have a kill criteria, meaning that, at the start, you will give yourself a deadline in pursuit of a goal for when it is time to walk away from a date deadline, money spent, results, numbers, and any other metric that confirms it is a good time to walk. Hikers on Mount Everest all have these, and no matter how high they have climbed, they must adhere to the kill criteria deadline. The 1996 Everest climb disaster was an example when a hiking group under the leadership of New Zealander Rob Hall did not follow clear deadlines, resulting in the deaths of four members of his expedition, including Hall himself.

Wise counsel is also essential when you are at a fork in the road and are fighting your own mind games about a goal or project and whether to continue on. Find a worthy mentor who can provide non-biased advice and who has your best interests at heart. They are worth their weight in gold.

Contrary to what most people think, quitting is not all bad and is an essential skill to learn and master as you make your way through life.

Multiple identities

The more interests and identities you have, the stronger you become

Having a diverse range of interests, hobbies and friendships is your best safety net

You are not your work or relationships

I once worked at an organisation where one of the long-time senior leaders got made redundant while I was there. This was a complete shock and came from left field to the man made redundant.

The now former leader took the news terribly and couldn't believe that he had been let go by the company. He really thought he was irreplaceable and would be in the role until he left or retired. This person's whole life was focused on the organisation; it was his life, as he had no other hobbies or interests outside his job.

A few months later, I unexpectedly ran into this man and I was stunned how far he had fallen in such a short space of time. The man's confidence and self belief had completely gone. They had been attached to his identity, and his status had been aligned to the former position, and now that this has been removed, he felt he was nothing and had sunk into deep depression and despair.

He looked a mess: his body language was poor, he looked emotionally and physically drained, and he radiated very little energy. He stated that his life was over and he even wondered and inquired of me if they might take him back in due course.

That man's sad story is one that is very common and one I have seen often in the corporate world, as well as couples after a divorce, or sports stars who become lost post retirement when their identity is no longer relevant.

If we are not to fall victim to that downward spiral that executive went through or the spiral that many sports stars go through once they finish their sporting careers, we must develop multiple identities that we can fall back on when times get tough. The reason that people, including so many sports stars and divorcees, fall so hard when something ends is that their whole identity and status is linked to that relationship or function they were performing.

The answer is to develop multiple identities and interests in our lives, so when one falls down, we have other areas that can pick us up. Not only will multiple identities help us during tough periods in our lives but they make our lives so much more interesting, adventurous and meaningful. We are so much more than our identity, which can sometimes only lead to pain and suffering.

Multiple identities

Identities that we can develop include our career, friendships, family relationships, our health, sports, reading and learning, travelling, joining a club, volunteering and pursuing other hobbies and interests, which make our lives more rounded and balanced.

This is not about being famous or making money — it's about being a well-balanced individual who is well read, well travelled, has a diverse range of interests and hobbies, and has built some deep relationships.

Having built those sorts of identities, we will be much stronger, flexible and adaptable when the winds of change and adversity come blowing into our lives. Rather than being capsized by events, we will be calm and serene, and ride the strong waves to the calm waters with what we have become.

Know where you are - keep score

If you don't know where you are, how can you get to where you want to be?

Take stock of your position

Responsibility is the mark of maturity

Once you get out to sea, all those waves look alike

Do you know where you are? Often, it takes an experience of great adversity or failure for us to realise we are not in a good position and we must change our course fast.

If you don't know where you are, how can you get to where you want to go?

This is a simple question but one that is the utter truth and worth thinking about. I learned this the hard way many times through life, often when I have been mindlessly going through the motions, losing focus, or thinking I was doing far better than I actually was, before some disaster struck and woke me up.

Know where you are - keep score

Life has a funny way of hitting you hard when you're not prepared.

You see this all around when health crises emerge in our lives, financial problems, relationship breakdowns, business failures, or the station we thought we would be in life and where we actually are compared to those past dreams and hopes.

Gaining weight, becoming bankrupt or having no money, marriage breakdown or business failure are rarely single events, but rather, a process over a period of time.

Once, I put on some pants that I had not worn for a while and I noticed they were far too tight. At first, I made the excuse that they must have shrunk in the wash, but it wasn't until I jumped on the scales after not doing so for a while that I quickly found out that those pants had not changed but I had, by putting on 10 kg. While it was not nice to see the higher numbers that meant weight gain, it did free me from false beliefs and perceptions. I was carrying 10 kg more than I had previously, and I now knew where I was and where I needed to be.

This had also occurred to me when not paying close enough attention to my finances. A few times I went overseas and was a little reckless with spending, and when I did check my bank statement, I was surprised how much money I had spent. I needed to rein it in to avoid later financial problems.

Sadly, most people have no idea where they are in life and have no real plan or goal for where they want to be! Most people are just drifting along aimlessly, and the faster they go, the quicker they get lost in confusion and anxiety with the stresses of life.

Sailors who sail the great seas say the waves all look alike after you leave the port and they must know where they are if they are to set a course and path.

Before any journey, any person would take stock of where they are and what route they need to take to reach their desired destination. Our lives are no different.

We live in a world where many people look to others to provide for and protect them, be it government, family or workplace. Responsibility is the highest mark of maturity in any individual, and only by taking full responsibility can we free ourselves and find internal freedom and peace of mind.

Security does not come from some external source such as a job, money or investments, which can all be lost very easily, but real security comes from within, developing the traits to weather the storms of life. Taking responsibility is at the top. No one is coming to save or help us and it is up to each of us to take charge and take responsibility for our lives and design the life we want.

Take stock of where you are in your life, because no one else is going to do this for you. We can measure and monitor many key elements in our life, from finances, health, decisions, investments, knowledge, books read, personal growth, businesses or whatever is important to us.

You can't improve something if you don't know where you are, and tracking progress, though sometimes painful, has many benefits. First, the numbers don't lie and they show us where we are, and secondly, they provide awareness of where we are and what we need to do to stay on track or get back on track.

Where are you with your health, your finances, vocation, relationships, hobbies, goals and dreams? It's your crop to harvest, so take good care of it, as it's the only one you have. Taking stock of where you are and getting the brutal facts may be painful at first if we have let things slide like I had done, but it's far worse if we don't check. That road only leads to regret and disappointment, two of the most bitter pills to swallow for anyone.

Keeping score and tracking our progress is one of the best tools to monitor our progress and keep us on course and avoid the dangers in life.

Gratitude

Give thanks always

Write down three things you're grateful for every day and you'll feel much better

Gratitude and its benefits for finding inner peace, contentment and happiness has been written about for thousands of years and goes as far back as the Bible and various other religions from both the East and West, to the many modern thinkers today. But like most good things, we need continual reminding of what we have previously learned.

Thousands of studies from all around the world have unanimously confirmed the benefits of gratitude to not only our lives but our health and mindset. We live in an age of excessive anxiety, stress, depression and other ailments, but often gratitude is the missing link to prevent us from falling into despair and to finding contentment and inner peace, no matter how bad life may be.

Australia and many other Western and Eastern countries over the last fifty years have seen wealth and living standards that many other countries could only dream about. But despite

Gratitude

this surge in living standards, unhappiness is more common than possibly any other era in history, with a pandemic of depression, anxiety and other mental and physical ailments. Money can help with happiness but it alone can't make you happy. Happiness can only be found from within and there really is no magic pill that some promise.

Too often, we look back at the past with regret and disappointments, and we also look forward to the future with apprehension, when all we have is the present moment.

Gratitude is the ground and foundation that can keep our lives in check and remind us of all the good things that we have in our lives.

One of the greatest sins in the modern world is ingratitude, and we have all been guilty of this great sin at one time or another. We take for granted people, infrastructure and inventions that others built, and the many who have come before us and paid the greatest price of death in war which gives us the freedoms we have today.

Just writing down three things every day that you are grateful for will have a tremendous impact on not only your thoughts and feelings but your outlook on life, and take you away from the self sabotaging habit of being worried only about yourself, which leads to misery and unhappiness. "At the very best, a person completely wrapped up in himself makes a small package," as Ben Franklin once said.

We have much to be happy for, including food, housing, family and friends, clothes, money, cars, computers, music, travel, books, sport, and roads, and we need reminding to be grateful for these wonderful blessings. Just start writing every day and you will see so much of the good in our lives. Energy flows where our mind goes, and gratitude leads to the good rather than what we don't have.

Gratitude puts us in a positive paradigm, as we think and feel better and then radiate positive energy, which others see and feel. Becoming grateful on a daily basis is one of the best habits we can all develop.

Give graciously and without fanfare

Give and you shall receive

What can I give?

It's a great blessing to be able to give

To pay our fair share of rent to the world we inhabit, I think it's imperative that we give in return for what the world has given to us and what others who have come before us have done, and ensure the future is better for all once we depart this world.

To pay our share of rent, we need to give, and, with our minds, there is no limit on how we can give back to the people and the world.

We can donate to charities or causes we support, volunteer, teach, help students or the elderly, support communities and clubs, be supportive to a work colleague, or something as simple as saying hello to a stranger or giving a friendly smile to someone walking on the street.

What we give out always comes back. We just feel better when we give. Study after study has proven this to be true. Great joy comes from when we give, no matter how small. Giving is the best way to get our focus off ourselves, when so often it can be selfish, and unto others, which puts our problems into real perspective. Energy flows where our awareness goes, and focusing on others is positive energy.

The fastest way to lighten your own load is to get your mind off yourself and start giving to others.

Giving graciously and without fanfare is a win-win for all parties and makes the world a better place.

Let's be the change we want to see in the world. It all starts with us, and giving, in any manner, no matter how small, is the best way we can return to the world what has been given to us and pay our fair share of rent, and let's do it with no fanfare.

Discontent can be healthy

There is no limit and there is no end
- William E Bailey

Gratitude is a wonderful thing and is one of the best habits we can each develop in our lives, but we also need to balance this with the understanding that discontent is totally normal and quite healthy.

Moments of complete bliss and satisfaction are wonderful but very rare and are only temporary feelings and soon give way to a nagging sensation of discontent.

The young often want to be old and the old young, the rested want work and the workers want relaxation, when around people for too long we long for solitude, and when alone we want company.

We think if we meet our dream partner, get our dream house or car or find riches, that we will find inner peace and happiness, but this is not true, and one only has to reflect on one's own life to observe the passing feelings that often lead to discontent.

Discontent is completely normal with our nature and behaviours and you can be assured it will always be coming throughout the seasons of your life. It comes with the territory of being human.

There is no limit and there is no end and we should never be happy or satisfied with our lives and should always be inspired to go to new and higher levels.

If you have discontent, that is a great thing, despite what we are told. Dissatisfaction is a creative state and provides emotional inner drive to fuel our lives. It's completely normal and we should harness it for good.

If you don't like it, change it - you're not a tree

For things to change you have to change
- Jim Rohn

The definition of insanity is doing the same thing over and over and expecting a different outcome
- Albert Einstein

So many times, we hear the complaints and whining from both ourselves and others which at times can drive both parties nuts when they are never-ending, when we have a problem-oriented outlook that can be based on playing the victim in life.

As blunt as it can be, if we don't like something, then we must change it, fix it and take full responsibility. Luckily, we are not a tree or fixed object and have been given the power of choice, and we can change the direction of our lives if we don't like it at any time.

I have often needed to be reminded of this throughout my life, from living in unhealthy environments after whinging for months, quitting jobs that were not good for me, making decisions to get my health and finances back on track, removing bad influences in my life, and many more life decisions that we are called on to navigate and make.

How in the world could we get a different outcome to our problems if we keep repeating the same actions over and over? Einstein said the definition of insanity was doing the same thing over and over again and expecting a different outcome. For things to change, we've got to change, and the beginning of any change is personal growth and becoming more. When we change and grow, our lives become better, and problems have a way of withering away as we outgrow what once was.

You're not a tree, and if you don't like stuff in your life, change it. It's a hell of a lot easier than whinging and whining and doing nothing.

Change, the remedy for an anxious and worried mind

Change is the master key

The mind is its own place, and in itself can make a heaven of hell, a hell of heaven
- John Milton, Paradise Lost

The mind can be worn out, just like clothes can be from daily wear and tear

Few people in the world have experienced more pressure than what Winston Churchill was under when he was Prime Minister of England during World War Two, when the country was at war with Nazi Germany, and in the early years of the war, things were looking very bleak for the British.

Churchill was able to stand up to the crisis and problems that would have destroyed most other men, with a system he developed earlier in his life for relieving worry and tension.

That key for Churchill was change!

Change was the master key, as a man can wear out parts of his mind with worry and doubt by continually using it, just like clothes can be worn out with overuse.

It is impossible to switch off and not continue to worry or be stressed, but if we activate other areas of our brain with change and other activities, we can be renewed, rested and strengthened.

The key is we must activate living cells in the brain that are not being used. Tired parts of the brain can be rested and renewed by using other parts of it.

Trying to shut down your brain when it is worried and anxious is virtually impossible, and only by turning it to something new, can new brain cells be called into activity. Switching off will not work, as you probably already know, as the worry and anxiety just lingers on and does not go away.

Churchill used active change to take his stresses and worries away by painting, gardening, sculpting, reading, listening to music, socialising and walking, and we can also use change to our advantage to take our own anxiety, stresses and worries away.

I, like Churchill, have used change to my advantage when worry and stress come my way, by activating new unused brain cells by performing different activities such as playing squash or other sports, high intensity exercise, playing or listening to music and just getting my mind to be active in a new area when one area is worn out with overuse.

Change, the remedy for an anxious and worried mind

It is a sort of magical thing that worry can just disappear when you start to do something completely different from whatever had you so worried and stressed before.

You can be a spectator at a sporting or music event and still worry, but you can't play and worry, and that is why active change in a new field is such a good remedy for worry and anxiety.

The trick to remove anxiety and worry is to force yourself to do something else when your mind is full of worry or tired from one form of work, especially when it is between the ears.

Churchill did this during the darkest days of World War Two to survive and thrive, and you can also. It's the best medical prescription for any form or worry, doubt and stress.

It's not overwork that kills people, as some say, but over-worry and stress are where the real harm comes from that leads to all kinds of health issues and eventually death.

You will find once you force your mind to move into a completely new activity from what you were doing and which had you anxious and worried, you will come back to the thing that had you worried, rested, renewed, refreshed, and sharper, and be in a much better frame of mind to resolve the problem and move forward.

Take a lesson from Churchill and use active change when facing your own worries and doubts. It's the best medicine you can take.

Peace of mind - develop yourself fully is the only way

No amount of money can ever buy peace of mind

Peace of mind comes from the full development of us as beings

Discontent is unfulfilled potential

To be, or not to be: that is the question
- Shakespeare (Hamlet, Act 3, Scene 1)

Many believe that peace of mind can only come from security, which includes having a nice home and car, some money in the bank or investment fund, stable family life, and a secure job. Whilst these are all nice, I don't believe they can bring real peace of mind to us as individuals.

To my thinking, real peace of mind can only come from the full development of ourselves as individuals. If we feel we have reached our potential and achieve some big goals that make us feel proud, we will generally feel pretty good about ourselves and those achievements, which leads to inner peace.

Viktor Frankl, author of *Man's Search for Meaning,* believed that our health depended on the natural tension that comes from comparing what we've accomplished so far in life with what we'd like to achieve in the future. What we need then is not a peaceful existence, but a challenge that we can strive for and that applies all the skills and talents at our disposal, one that gives our life meaning and purpose and does not lead to an existential crisis that so many confront today. Frankl's creation of logotherapy was all about helping one find purpose and meaning in life and help an individual fill an existential void.

Peace of mind doesn't only come from achieving what we set out to do, but also from developing our virtues and character traits. You can't have peace of mind without a clear conscience, and both are necessary for real peace of mind.

Discontent is on the other side of the coin, and we can say that our level of dissatisfaction is a good indicator of our level of peace of mind. The more dissatisfaction we have in our lives, the less peace of mind we have. Regret, fears, worry and doubt have a funny way of creating internal rift, and the solution is to become all we can be. On this journey of striving, growing, learning and becoming, we find peace of mind.

If we have put off or not gone after what we know we should do or really desire and want, we are certain to hear that nagging voice of discontent. Use discontent and know that it can be a signal for your life that you are off track and that unless you go after your true and real desires, your calling or what some may call your destiny, you will never find peace of mind.

Excellence

We are what we repeatedly do... therefore excellence is not an act, but a habit
- Will Durant, after Aristotle

Excellence always sells
- Earl Nightingale

Quality over quantity

Perfection is not attainable, but if we chase perfection we can catch excellence
- Vince Lombardi

Excellence is doing ordinary things extraordinarily well
- John W Gardner

There is only one way you will stand out in life and that is to develop the art of excellence in any work you perform, no matter how big or small.

James B Conant, when president of Harvard University, said each honest calling, each walk of life has its own elite, its own aristocracy, based upon excellence of performance.

There is an elite in any field or profession, from the trades, chefs, salespeople, writers, artists, musicians, engineers, lawyers, furniture makers, doctors, dentists, builders, accountants and every professional imaginable.

William Shakespeare, John Steinbeck, Ernest Hemingway, Jane Austen, Albert Einstein, Thomas Edison, Michelangelo, Leonardo Da Vinci, Vincent Van Gogh, Michael Jordan, Tiger Woods, Michael Phelps, Bob Dylan, and Bruce Springsteen all reached the top of their chosen fields through the relentless pursuit of excellence and quality.

Some of the biggest global business brands have stood at the top due to enduring quality, such as Apple, Rolls Royce, Toyota and Amazon.

We see it all around us locally, with a restaurant that always delivers quality food and has excellent reviews, groundsmen who have the sporting ground in immaculate condition for the big game, metal or furniture workers who pride themselves on excellence with customers, the baker who is in demand from mothers in her community for her kids' birthday cakes, or the builder who has a huge backlog of work after rave reviews for his building quality with new homes.

The respect for excellence never changes and there is always space at the top. The bottom is where it is crowded. We all love quality and should demand it, from where we eat and shop, and by what we produce and create. We should also demand it from ourselves and do the best we can.

One way to find if you are in the right field is to ask yourself if you care about the quality of your finished work. If you really care, this is one of the strongest signs that you are in work that interests and stimulates you, and you care very much about the quality, presentation and final product. If you don't care about the quality of your work, this is a very strong sign you're in work that has little meaning, purpose or enjoyment, and you should consider looking at something else that provides more meaning and purpose.

The benefits of excellence are many, including quickly becoming a leader in your chosen field. The elite of any profession are never short of work or opportunity and are always in demand, as excellence never goes out of fashion. But maybe more important is the psychic income you will receive from doing your work to the best of your ability with the highest quality. You will radiate many positive emotions, including personal satisfaction, joy and pride, and continue the process of continual learning and growth.

The dedication to excellence will separate you from your peers and competitors. Doing our best should be our motto for anything in life. Excellence always has a seat at the table.

Turn disgust into inspiration

That's it. Never again

The day that turns your life around
- Jim Rohn

Decisions, as discussed in a previous chapter, are one of the greatest powers that lie within each of us, and that power, unfortunately, lies dormant far too often.

Never is this more apparent than when we are faced with a major adversity or challenges that seem overwhelming.

When most people face great obstacles or adversity, they too often roll over and give up, but there is a small group who turn that disgust about what has become of their life as great motivation for inspiration.

It could be a job loss, business failure, a girlfriend or wife/husband has left you for another, rejection, bankruptcy, house eviction, weight gain, drinking your life away, staying in a job you hate, or maybe life is just not where you expected it would be when you were much younger, with the once great hopes and aspirations having now evaporated in the face of the brutal reality of life and routine.

Turning disgust into inspiration is one of the greatest philosophies I have learned on the road of life. It's where we turn the scenario around, and, rather than crawl away and succumb to our failures and the ugly lot in life we find ourselves in, we reverse the situation and use disgust as inspiration and fuel to get out of the ugly situation we are in and use that energy to change our life completely.

We should welcome all experiences and emotions, and some of those ugly experiences and feelings can be catalysts for the day that turns our life around — the moment when you say, That's it! I will not live without money, stay in a job I hate, accept business failure or rejection from outsiders, not be able to walk the stairs or fit into my pants. These can be moments that we say, "No more! I will not let this situation define my life! Rather than become a victim, I will use these emotions of disgust as inspiration to turn my life around."

Disgust can be one of the most powerful emotions that fuels our life. We should welcome all experiences and emotions, both bad and good. You never know when could be the day that turns your life around and changes you — a pivotal moment when, rather than becoming the victim, through disgust, you channel those emotions to become a greater being and rise up and become greater than before the adversity you faced.

Each of us is greater than any of our problems, and the minute we stop being the victim or giving in to our terrible lot in life is the moment we take charge and control the steering wheel of our lives.

Turn disgust into inspiration

Disgust is one of the most powerful emotions, and when we flip the situation in our favour and turn that disgust into inspiration, it is one of the most powerful moments in any person's life.

Welcome all experiences and emotions. You never know what will be the moment that changes your life forever.

Confidence comes from knowledge

Competence and confidence come from experience

I once managed a small team, and one member of the team was quite new to the workforce and was only twenty years old. This young woman was very polite and well mannered but she lacked the vital quality of confidence to be able to perform the job.

Over the next six months, as with many young people starting out in their careers, she made many mistakes, and, during a review, it was clear she was struggling with many functions of the role and needed more support.

I told her: "The reasons why you are struggling and lacking confidence is you don't know the role as well as you should. There are some functions which you know well and you are very confident in, but for other functions, which you struggle in, you lack confidence, which impacts your competence."

After the review, we focused on what she needed to improve in the role, and, over the next six months, this young woman really matured and grew into the role and became very competent and effective. This was largely from knowing how to perform the job.

When she first started, I would notice many errors, and then we would have to go back over those mistakes and provide more training. But once she started to really know the role and didn't need to ask for any assistance or support, then her confidence shot up like a rocket. She never looked back and ended up growing too big for the role.

That is the power of knowledge that equates to confidence, when one really knows what one is doing and has the inner confidence that is developed after years of practice and study, of learning and failure and understanding in any field what quality looks like and what the customer likes.

Many people talk about faking confidence, but the only authentic confidence comes from knowledge and experience. The examples are endless, from driving a car, cooking a meal, knowing how to lead and manage, and skilled tradespeople of all types who know how to fix a problem.

If one is lacking confidence, often all that is missing is knowledge and experience. Once one gains both of those critical elements, confidence and competence are sure to follow.

Dealing with uncertainty

No one knows for sure what tomorrow will bring
- Bible (James 4:14)

Embrace uncertainty to grow and become
a greater soul for you and others

Pave your own path

When uncertainty and problems come, call them
projects or adventures to help you face them

The fear and worry of the unknown lives
and dies in the imaginary mind

The same wind blows on us all; the winds of
disaster, opportunity and change. Therefore, it is
not the blowing of the wind, but the setting of the
sails that will determine our direction in life
- Jim Rohn

One thing you are sure to face in your life is uncertainty. Uncertainty is the unknown or the road where we don't know where it goes or what is going to happen next, and it is very uncomfortable for most people. It's the complete opposite to security and comfort that one most longs for and has left many destitute in fear and worry throughout history.

Dealing with uncertainty

The fear of the unknown is perhaps the greatest of all fears we all may face in our lives. An important fact, though, is it's not even real, and it lives and dies in the mind only.

Uncertainty has been a common presence and thorn throughout my life. How you respond to such times will play a huge role in how your life turns out and who you become as a person.

Like many subjects discussed in this book, no one in school or the workplace ever discussed how we will all face great times of uncertainty in our lives. That is incredible when you come to realise how much we don't know about what will happen in our lives and how much is uncertain, with constant change throughout one's life and the world we inhabit.

Uncertainty has come often into my life, from not having a rental house and not knowing where I will live, being made redundant and not knowing what to do next for work, financial pressures of all kinds, career and business uncertainty, and external threats such as COVID, which impacted millions around the world during the pandemic.

Times of uncertainty can be some of the most destructive and stressful periods in our lives, with both internal and external threats, from housing, relationships, changes of all types, career and business, money problems that can cause great periods of stress and uncertainty. They can also come from such events as war, famines, floods and other weather events, social issues, a changing world, political issues, economic issues, pandemics, cyber attacks, and other matters that impact us all.

How you respond to uncertainty will define whether it controls you with fear, doubt and worry, or whether you manage to sail the winds of change and the unknown with calmness, direction and poise.

Some tips I have learned when dealing with uncertainty are to develop stoic character traits and to always remember you can only control what you can control. Often, only doing what you can do at this very moment is the best you can do in any situation, where many things and events are out of your control. Doing all that you can do and what needs to be done each day is often the best action and strategy in any period of uncertainty. Looking for another job, finding a new house or rental, saving money where you can, apologising if there is a relationship breakdown, and reading and gathering information to support and educate you are all types of actions one can do in times of uncertainty. It's also wise to become aware of what is outside of your control, rather than burning emotional energy when you can do little about what is concerning you.

Build options and diversity into your life, so if one thing falls down, you have other forms of insurance to help you out. Having all your eggs in one basket can be a disaster when that option is no longer helpful. Having options is the greatest form of life insurance for any individual, and we can build this into our lives by saving money, having alternative career options and skills if one sector or industry fails, starting a side hustle, changing our perceptions, knowing other key people if one person lets us down or is unavailable, having insurances and different forms of investments to shield us against any disaster. We can also try many small bets and then follow through with the big winners that show promise.

Being adaptable to changing times and situations, all positions in life are temporary is a key law. The only thing for certain in life is change, so be flexible, nimble and adaptable to periods of change and uncertainty. You may have to change roads and think and do things differently, and what once worked may not work now — you may need to forge a new path into the unknown. So don't be too structured. What may have worked once may not work in the present and future.

Read how many have encountered and dealt with times of uncertainty, from the Greek tragedies; Homer's epic story *The Odyssey; The Baghavad Gita; In a Far Country* by Jack London; the Old Testament story of Job; *The Grapes of Wrath* by John Steinbeck, set during the Great Depression; *Lonesome Dove* by Larry McMurtry, *The Road* by Cormac McCarthy; and, finally, Victor Frankl's *Man's Search for Meaning*, which recalls his time in a Nazi concentration camp during World War Two. These are just a number of great reads on stories of struggle and uncertainty that can inspire and help you deal with your own struggles in times of doubt, worry and uncertainty.

Remain calm and collected. As discussed, "calmness" is my favourite word in the English language, and in times of uncertainty, calmness will be your best friend to keep your emotions in check. The ability to keep your head and remain calm and serene when everyone around you is losing theirs with panic, fear and stress will make you stand out as a leader and person who can be counted on in a crisis. The ability to stay calm no matter which way the winds are blowing is one of the greatest traits we can all nurture and develop.

Change your perception of uncertainty, rather than seeing something as a great threat during periods of uncertainty like most people do, which can often cause fear, stress, doubt and worry. Flip the switch and look at this period or situation of uncertainty in a different light. I have looked at it as a growth opportunity, adventure or project that has had a huge positive effect, when I have faced my own perilous times of uncertainty. Know that this period of uncertainty will pass and is just a temporary situation.

Lastly, embrace periods of uncertainty and let the stories of the past inspire you to become a greater being when facing your own internal and external threats. The Greatest Generation, who went through the Great Depression and World War Two, faced incredible threats and long periods of uncertainty and yet came out the other side stronger and wiser and became respected as the greatest generation of all. You, like them, are greater than any threat, challenge, change or period of uncertainty you will face, and you can thrive in uncertainty.

Uncertainty, while uncomfortable and stressful to all of us, is one of the best adversities any person can face for personal growth and maturity. We must remember that uncertainty is sure to be encountered on our journey through life, and we can set the sail no matter which way the winds blow. We will come through the other side, no matter what may come our way, and, in the process, grow and become more.

All problems are temporary

It's just a temporary situation

When we get better, life gets better

Intellect annuls fate
- Ralph Waldo Emerson

In an earlier lesson, we talked about a fundamental law that all positions in life are temporary. The cousin law to this essential law is that all problems are also temporary.

Problems will always arise throughout our lives, and we can often be bombarded with challenges when issue after issue keeps arising and we feel like there's no way out of the mess that we are in. But problems, like positions and stations throughout life, are all temporary, and we should never lose sight of this law, no matter how bleak things may seem or the vast size of the mountain and challenges we are facing off against.

Problems seem to be a part of life, and to go to the next level we must find answers to our problems. Only by finding solutions to our problems can we keep growing and becoming more.

All problems are temporary

Throughout our lives, we will face many problems, from relationships, finances, career, health, business, world events, the unexpected, and many other things.

Strangely, despite the importance of resolving problems in our lives, I have never received any training on resolving problems. I was never taught this in school or the workplace. This skill is usually developed only when we face great challenges.

Often, our heads are chaotic with over thinking and can be bombarded with noise and over-stimulation from a vast array of media sources.

To solve any problem, we first need to get it out of our head and onto paper. We need to define what the problem is. Just doing this first step will bring much more clarity to our thoughts and the problem we are facing.

Half the answer to any problem is first defining it. The next step is to take some quiet time alone and think of all the solutions to our problem, and write anything down, even those outrageous ideas and thoughts. Sometimes the answer may not come immediately, but one of the greatest and often dormant powers is our subconscious mind, which can go to work and find answers even whilst we are asleep. The subconscious is an incredible tool and has unlimited power, including the power to solve any problem. The incredible thing is, it goes to work on our problems even if we are not thinking about them. Many stories have been told about how ideas and solutions came to people from nowhere, who at one point seemed at a loss about how to solve their problems.

Solving problems is one of the greatest skills any person could develop, and, just like any skill, it takes practice and time to get better. There is an old saying that life gets better when we get better, and that really is true.

The 1, 2, 3 combo of defining our problem by writing it down, and then letting our mind look at all angles for solutions, and finally turning it over to our subconscious, has lifted many to overcome impossible odds. It can be done for both you and me.

All problems are temporary in life and we should never lose sight of this. There is a solution to any problem, and often we need to get out of our chaotic thinking and put it down on paper with some quiet time to clear our minds and really define what the problem is.

Having options

Having options is the best life insurance policy available

*You are the sum total of your thoughts,
beliefs and choices at this moment*

Plan for the worst but hope for the best

One of the best life lessons I have learned along the road of life is to try and have and build options with life itself to make the trip easier. Options are incredible in their benefit, but the lack of options is the complete opposite and can cause all sorts of problems.

Lack of options can cause incredible stress and pressure in one's life. I remember once when my rental lease ended and I could not find another house. The lack of alternative rental options caused enormous stress for me. I was close to being on the streets, having no other option available. I have seen this in other areas of my life also, including, for example, with looking for a job when out of work. When you only have one job interview, you are putting all your hopes on that one role and you end up interviewing badly, as you put so much pressure on yourself to get the job. Yet, when you have many interviews and options, you are far more relaxed and tend to perform much better and have better results.

You see this with the guy who has put all his life on trying to win over one girl, but in the process, his neediness turns her off him. Having many options with many different girls at one time, the guy tends to be far more relaxed and so he attracts more interested women, and eventually gets the one he wants. Having options may be counterintuitive in a way, but many people have noticed that they perform better when they have other choices. I think this is due to the relaxed and calm state we are in, where we fear and worry less about the outcome.

Having options in an ever-changing world is a necessary skill and life hack to develop and build throughout one's life, especially in the digital age, where we have seen the rise of globalisation and AI, which has meant many jobs going to China, India and the Philippines, and modern technology replacing many roles. Having six months of savings gives you time to find the next opportunity and not feel threatened by your boss or being out of work. Learning new skills gives you alternative options. If you find yourself out of work in your current field, continual study in another field gives you more opportunity in the future.

Being able to move across states or countries can provide enormous opportunities if your region or country is lacking opportunities. Having a back-up housing option takes the stress away if you are forced to leave your rental or home for any reason. Just like having a spare set of keys for your

Having options

house in case you lose one set, build options and back-up plans into all areas of your life for when emergencies or the unexpected do arise, from money, investments, career, skills, insurances, friendships, living environment, housing, cars, knowledge base, and other essential living requirements. Building these options will make you antifragile and far stronger. You will manage a crisis far better when you have solid alternative options.

Always plan ahead, as life will never go to plan. It can be wise to plan for the worst but hope for the best and have some options to ride out the storms of life.

Creative thinking

Thinking is the hardest work

Think and grow rich
- Napoleon Hill

Excellence is not an act but a habit
- Aristotle

Earl Nightingale said that thinking was the hardest work but is a necessity if we are to live our best life.

Throughout my life, I have been told what to think and do but never have I been taught how to think. It's quite incredible that most of us go through school, university and the workplace and receive no training whatsoever on how to think — no training on how to use our marvellous minds!

Sadly, very few people do any form of real creative thinking and most blindly follow the masses or conform to society.

There is no doubt that creative thinking is hard work, but we must make time to use the most precious gift we have been given — our human mind.

Take some quiet time away from all the noise of life to think creatively on how to improve your life and the lives of others.

Creative thinking

Make it a regular part of your life and schedule. It's a skill that can be learned with enough practice, just like any other skill.

Everything we see in the world was once in the mind of someone. The key was to act on the ideas they had.

Ask questions, stimulate dialogue, reflect on your life, ask how can you serve more to get a better return, how can you solve the problems you face, how can you improve and make yourself more valuable to others and yourself?

All change starts in the mind, and creative thinking is essential if we are to reach our potential and utilise all that we have been given. Our health, finances, relationships, new ideas, lifestyle, homelife, and society can all be improved with regular thinking time.

Your mind is better than any gold mine. Take some time to mine it and you will find plenty of gold.

Take risks

No risk, no gain

You can't get to second base with one foot on first base

We should remove the word "security" from our vocabulary

If we are to reach our full potential and put fear, doubt and worry behind us, we must learn to take risks that help us move to the next level for whatever goals and desires we have.

When we talk about risks, we are not talking about being totally reckless but about knowing ourselves, what we want from life and taking bold action to get there.

One of the great regrets of the dying is that they wish they took more risks and lived more. So much wisdom comes from that sentence alone for us who still have a chance to live and take risks.

Many of the dying regret not asking that girl out, quitting the job they hated and starting their own business, leaving the city for the quiet life, starting a new career, fighting for their marriage, travelling to places that they had always

Take risks

wanted to go, taking time to cultivate friendships and many other things.

Risks are good for us and make life more exciting and we should not shy away from making some bold moves in our lives, no matter what our stage of life is.

Let's take the attitude that new frontiers, new boundaries and new adventures are waiting to be found. Uncertainty brings excitement and makes us feel more alive.

We all need adventure

Life is a daring adventure or nothing at all
- Helen Keller

When you look back at some of the greatest men and women to have ever lived throughout history, those who have achieved incredible success and lived lives others could only dream about, they all shared one key trait: a passion to live a romantic and adventurous fun-filled life.

Jack London, Teddy Roosevelt, Winston Churchill, Edmund Hillary, Ronald Reagan, Ernest Hemingway, and Amelia Earhart are just a few who had this unique passion to go out and live an adventurous, romantic, fun-filled life, and their stories should inspire us all to follow in their footsteps and squeeze everything we can out of life.

They packed decades into years and centuries into decades, and we can do the same with our own lives if we have the same attitude towards seeking adventure.

Sadly, this romanticism and adventurous lust for life has been lost in the modern world with gadgets and apps, and the majority of the world living stationary boring lives that have

We all need adventure

zapped the passion and zest for life, as billions have become addicted to screen time and social media likes.

Schooling and work are often mundane and repetitive, and the idea of adventure is foreign to many today. Unless someone gets it from their parents or from some other form of stimulation or experience, they will not seek out adventure.

We need adventure. It's not only great for the soul, but our inner being is dying for adventure and the unknown and wants to be unleashed. We were born for adventure and we should chase it until our dying days.

Developing a romantic and adventurous attitude for life comes from our minds and spirits, and its opportunities are only limited by our thinking. All it takes is opening our minds and spirits to the world around us. All the adventure we could ever want is already here, waiting to be discovered.

Italy, New Zealand, Spain, Iceland, Ireland, Norway, Scotland, Namibia, Costa Rica, Morocco, Australia, South Africa, Botswana, Greece, Portugal, Germany, Japan, Thailand, Sri Lanka, Russia, Chile, Argentina, Peru, Fiji, the Cook Islands, Turkey, Argentina, America, Canada, the Caribbean and many other countries around the world have some of the most incredible things to do and see, and yet very few people have any real desire and passion to experience what the world has to offer and would prefer to be in front of a screen.

You don't need to travel around the world to have adventure. You could go on a road trip: hunting, fishing, hiking, and camping are all available to us. Adventure is nothing more than creating experiences that will last as memories for a lifetime.

If you live well, you will feel well and earn well, and more good things will come into your life. You will radiate passion and energy with your zest for life. It can only attract more good things to you.

Having a romanticism for adventure and life in general will reward you in ways no amount of money ever could. It is something I urge you to seek out.

Always have something to look forward to

The promise of the future is an awesome force
- William E Bailey

One of the best decisions you can ever make is to always have something to look forward to in life. That means planning adventures in advance and putting them on the calendar.

Not only do they provide inspiration, energy, and excitement, they can also pull you through the times when life is a slog and things are tough. All it requires is to plan in advance and put something on the calendar.

This philosophy has been one of the greatest blessings in my life. There have been many times when work or other matters have not been going great, but whenever I have something booked on the calendar, it pulls me through the hard times.

The promise of the future is an awesome force, and we should work with it to design an adventurous life that always gives us something to look forward to, with both mini and major adventures.

These don't have to be big trips, and can be anything, such as a day or weekend trip away, a hike, catching up with friends, visiting a new town, a nice relaxed drive, watching a concert, visiting a museum, attending a sports event or anything else that interests you.

Always have something to look forward to. It will pull you through the tough times and also make you a far more interesting person.

Everything which ever has been and ever will be is here now and can be discovered

I tell you: ask, and you shall receive; seek, and you shall find; knock, and the door shall be opened to you. For everyone who asks, receives; and everyone who seeks, finds; and to everyone who knocks, the door will be opened
- Jesus Christ (Matthew 7:7-8)

The supreme power can create - man can only construct and therein lies the difference
- William E Bailey

Are you aware that physical gold was here well before the gold rush seekers found gold in California and Victoria during the mid 19th century?

The ability to put a man on the moon was possible well before 1969.

Electricity was always here, long before Ben Franklin flew a kite.

Why then did we not find these things and many other great discoveries earlier? Maybe because we were not looking for them or knew that they were possible.

William E Bailey said that everything that ever has been and ever will be is here now and can be discovered! That mindset and philosophy really is the law of abundance and one we should all cultivate in our own lives and how we see the promise of the future.

All the money, knowledge, energy and truth has always been here, but it's up to each of us to get off our knees and find it. Everything we desire or want is here right now in one form or another and can be discovered. That should be a source of great encouragement.

Mankind can construct but only God can create and therein lies the difference. We should work with these universal laws and create with what is available in the world at our disposal.

We can only make steel from iron ore and gasoline from oil — we can't make a tree or energy but we can construct from what is already here now in the world.

Everything that we are seeking is here now and can be discovered but it's up to each of us to do our part and build from what already exists.

Knowing that everything is here now and can be discovered should give us great confidence, faith and belief that the future can be better and there is no limit to what we can achieve. Once you understand this you will be on the road to the millionaire mindset.

Character must be your foundation

Deeds not words
- George Washington

Be more concerned about your character than what others think of your reputation
- John Wooden

The Bible says to build your house on rock and not sand, so you will not be washed away when the storms of life come. Our rock for this life has to be our character in action.

Forget money, acquiring things, chasing status, owning a successful business, becoming a leader — all of these are pointless and worthless without character as our foundation and bedrock.

Throughout my life, I have seen those who have cheated, rorted, deceived with dishonest and unethical practices and behaviours have their world come tumbling down. Real success and happiness can only be achieved and maintained through having a sound foundation.

Character is the concrete of truth we must build our lives on, and, like most lessons in this book, I never received any tutorial from school or the workplace on its importance. I was told what to do and what not to do and think, but not what holds a life together and builds trust and respect from others. No one spoke about character and just how important it is, not only to ourselves but also our families and communities.

We are not born with character and it must be developed over a lifetime as we try to chisel away the bad habits that can often hold us back. Developing real character is definitely not the easiest task and is one I have struggled with throughout my life, like many others have.

We all know someone who has a shady character, from the dishonest salesman, the egotistical leader, the deceiver, the backstabber, the liar, the manipulator or the moral grandstanders that we see en masse today, who play moral guidelines about moral matters and yet their hearts are far away from these causes that they preach about.

Developing character as our foundation is a continual process over a lifetime and will require maintenance to our last breath.

To build our character, we must first take the time to define what will be the roots of our character, the characteristics we want to build our lives around. The characteristics have been spoken about throughout the ages, from ancient Greek philosophers such as Socrates, Plato and Aristotle, to Roman leader Marcus Aurelius, to the Bible, and many other famous men and women throughout the ages.

Character must be your foundation

These great men and women spoke about courage, integrity, compassion, honesty, duty and responsibility, all of which have never gone out of fashion or style.

Some of the traits I wanted to build my life on when I took the time to identify the key traits that would be needed to improve my character were: honesty, integrity, courage, confidence, compassion, loyalty, calmness, duty, discipline, taking responsibility, decisiveness, generosity, creativity, kindness, faith, and flexibility.

Take the time and define what you want to build your foundation on. It will hold you in good stead when the storms of life arrive and you remain strong, with sound foundations.

Courage - the finest of all values

Courage is the finest of all human values
- Winston Churchill

Some say knowledge is power, but it is not true. Character is power
- Sai Baba

Fear kills more people than death
- George Patton

The secret to happiness is freedom and the secret to freedom is courage
- Thucydides

One of the greatest human qualities that we can cultivate is courage. Churchill called it the finest of all human qualities. Many wartime leaders, famous sports coaches, politicians, business and community leaders who have excelled and gone through great trials and adversity in the process all talk about courage and how one can't succeed without it.

Unfortunately, in the cancel culture that has enveloped Western society where it seems everybody is a victim of some kind, the greatest of all qualities has been forgotten, with a wave of Socialism, Marxism and Communism spreading across the ecosystem.

Often, courage comes to the rescue in dire situations when there seems no hope: Churchill's brave stand against the Nazis in World War Two, Ronald Reagan against Communism and the Soviet Union, Harriet Tubman leading slaves to freedom on the underground railroad, Anne Frank and her family living in secret and quiet to hide from the Nazis, the police, firefighters and citizens who rushed into buildings to save lives on September 11, 2001, Sir Edmund Hillary's climb up Mount Everest, Americans fighting in the revolution and civil war, and many other examples.

Courage is not limited to those famous examples. Everyday people provide endless examples of great courage, from living life on their own terms and starting a new business, asking a girl out, moving to another city, starting a new career, making difficult decisions that will impact the lives of many, standing up for others when it is not popular, taking some great financial risk or chasing their dreams despite the criticism from friends and family who mock and taunt them.

Courage is essential if we are to live the life we want and on our terms. Fear of life has become the favourite disease of the mind this century. People are afraid of today and tomorrow, pessimistic about the future and seem to be worried and anxious about anything.

Courage is the antidote to fear and worry: the courage to do what is right and honourable, to be a leader in a crisis, and to have the courage to go after what we want for our lives, despite the critics and naysayers.

Never more than now do we and our countries need courage. It's within the reach of all of us, and without it, we have no foundation or freedom, as history has proven time and again.

Integrity - the number one quality for success and happiness

By their fruit you shall know them
- Bible (Matthew 7:16)

Integrity is everything

Society's rapid decline really is an integrity issue at its core

And if you think tough men are dangerous, wait until you see what weak men are capable of
- Jordan B. Peterson

What does a woman look for in a husband and a man in a wife, a patient in a dentist or doctor, or a customer with any business transaction or purchase?

The answer is one simple word — integrity.

We can never achieve or maintain success or happiness without integrity. Integrity is the number one requirement for both success and happiness and what we all look for from others.

We have all worked with bosses and colleagues who lack character and who lie, steal, cheat and cause division in the workplace, and we have all met the salesman who wants a quick profit and tries to rip us off financially or sell a product that can't do what it says.

Integrity is basically being honest and having strong moral principles that refuse to change, no matter what is thrown our way or what others say. It's the rock and foundation we build for our lives.

You would think a characteristic that holds so much importance would be taught in the schools, workplaces and at home, but in the overwhelming majority of cases, this is not taught or discussed.

Character matters, and who we become is more important than what we get. We have all met the people who have sold their soul for fame and wealth.

We see the consequences of lacking integrity everywhere, from government politicians and bureaucrats who lie, steal and cheat from the people and are involved in endless corruption scandals and cover-ups. The media can no longer be trusted today and push fake news to support financial backers with misinformation. Big Pharma rolled out vaccines without proper testing, resulting in many deaths and injuries, which has now been confirmed by independent authorities. Banks have created record asset bubbles across stocks, bonds and real estate, resulting in the worst cost of living crisis in over fifty years, while the banks make billions in profit with ruthless greed and care little for their own customers and fellow countrymen, who struggle in poverty, and academia who have brainwashed a generation of students with Marxist and Communist ideals that is causing endless division across society, where students want to destroy everything from the past and have a victim mindset throughout life, with no thought of self responsibility or integrity.

Our conscience is a funny thing. I have learned that it will quickly tell us when we are not acting with integrity or honour. We can never find true happiness without having integrity and treating all with respect and fairness. It's one of the worst feelings you can have when your conscience is telling you have done wrong to others, and it really makes you feel guilty and ashamed of your actions. I can attest to this many times and I am sure you can too.

Integrity really is everything, and although we all have character flaws, we have to work on our character like a sculptor who chisels away day after day, until our last day on Earth, to become a person who is honest, has clear moral guidelines, is fair and ethical, and others will say he is a person of integrity. That may be one of the highest aims we can all have for our lives.

We can never achieve and maintain success and happiness without integrity, so make it your foundation and work on it to your last breath.

Leadership

Everything falls and rises on leadership
- John Maxwell

Be the leader you wish you had
- Simon Sinek

The decline in the West over the last generation is strongly correlated to and a major reflection of the diminishing leadership capabilities in many Western countries. History has proven that at the head of any strong family, sporting team, organisation, business, government or country is always strong leadership. Everything falls and rises on leadership. With strong leadership, the results are strong, with poor leadership, the results are bad, and it flows downstream.

Leadership is one of the most noble qualities we can develop in our own lives. We may have no ambition to become a leader, but we should still take a keen interest in developing and honing our leadership skills. Leadership is required for leading ourselves, our families, our workplaces, our communities, government and countries, and every leader helps the greater good.

Leadership

I unfortunately have worked with far more bad leaders than good ones in my career, and, in fact, it has become very rare to find that brilliant leader who leaves an indelible mark and legacy.

We should all aim to be the leaders we wish we had in any environment.

Leadership development can include studying peers or idols whose leadership style and qualities you have admired from close and afar, how to set a direction and goal for any environment that you lead, how to communicate both verbally and in writing, how to work and lead people, how to look after and develop people under you and build and grow more leaders, how to take control of your emotions, how to make wise decisions, become more knowledgeable and handle crises when they arrive.

The development of your leadership skills in any capacity will increase your value and make you far more self confident, as well as flowing to other areas of your life. It's one of the best ways we can all improve ourselves and become better people, by developing and honing our leadership qualities.

Lead by example, judge by results

Everything is matter of opinion but results are real
- William E Bailey

You need results to be a success

Everything is a matter of opinion in life but results are real. My philosophy in my own life and when leading teams is to lead by example and judge by results.

Results are everything and we should always base our assessment or judgement on matters on results only, or we will be in for a huge amount of pain and disappointment.

We can quickly determine our results in life by simply judging the fruit and not what we or others say or think.

What are our current financial numbers, what is our current weight and how is our physical health, as well as our spiritual and emotional health, what is the health of our relationships, how many books have we read in the past year, what is the performance of the team we are leading, our home life, our career and business, our daily disciplines and our learning habits?

Lead by example, judge by results

Sometimes the results can be harsh and hard and not what we want, but they are needed if we are to stay on track and get the results we seek. Remember, only the truth will set us free.

Jesus made an unexpected point in the Bible about results when He asked the disciples one day, "Does this fig tree have any figs?" to which they said, "No. Of all the trees you were to pick, this particular fig tree does not have any figs." The story says that Jesus then lost His cool. This is one of the few times He ever became angry. He did it, I think, to make a point. A fig tree without figs is simply unacceptable. Jesus said, "If that fig tree doesn't have any figs, I suggest you promptly take it out!" Then He added, "Why let it take up the ground?"

Always remember everything is a matter of opinion but results are real.

Communication

Our words have the power to build people up and give them life or tear people down and bring them death
- Bible (Proverbs 18:21)

Learning how to communicate is one of the greatest skills we can learn and develop and is an essential life skill to help us work with others in any environment. In my life, I have found that business is easy and people are hard, and any way we can improve our communication and listening skills can only help us work with others.

Communication is not really taught in the school curriculum, and only a few workplaces train staff on this essential subject.

You must sell yourself to get the date, present well at the interview to get the job, persuade others to join your cause, and influence others about your ideas, and this all requires a solid foundation on how to speak, listen, write and communicate.

To become a great communicator, we need to get the basics down, and this starts with having something good to say and saying it well. It also involves knowing when to use more emotion, and reading and understanding your audience.

Communication

One of the best things we can all do to improve our communication and writing skills is to improve our command of the English language. All the great literature and speeches come from the 26 letters in the English language. Shakespeare, Hemingway, Steinbeck, Jefferson, Reagan, Lincoln, Churchill are just a few examples from history of writers and speakers who mastered the English language and used it with great command and mastery.

We must become great listeners who can pick people up on the emotional level and think and feel what they are feeling and saying.

The art of communication can open doors you never thought possible. It all starts with having a sound foundation of the basics. We may never become brilliant orators but we can all have a sound base to work from.

Earl Nightingale said the three key steps to basic communication and persuasion were to get the other party to listen to you first, then get them to understand what you are saying or selling, and then finally, to get them to act on what you want.

Having something good to say, being well read and having interesting life experiences will help you deal with people from all walks of life. Saying well what you have to say, becoming a great listener and knowing how to use other communication tools when needed, such as emotion, anger, story telling, facts and figures, will all help us navigate dealing with people and groups in many different environments.

Listening

True listening is an art

Listen and respond rather than hearing and reacting

God gave you two ears and one mouth

Our happiness and success in life greatly depends on our relationships and communications with others, yet what is one of the most important skills — how to communicate with others — is not taught in the school curriculum, and very few workplaces provide training for this essential life skill, as discussed in the last chapter.

At the core of any relationship and communication is the ability to be a really good listener. To really listen is an art form and takes many years of experience and putting others before yourself to master. I was often guilty, like most people, of not listening to the other person during a conversation and would only be concerned with what I wanted or was about to say rather than really listening to the other person on the emotional level.

Listening

Listening is essential to strengthen our friendships and relationships and having strong communication skills that can weave through topics and sensitive emotions.

Too many people today hear and react rather than listen and respond. That should be our foundation with understanding others: to listen and respond with care rather than react with impulse.

A student once asked a professor, "What is the key to good conversation?" The professor held up his finger and said, "Listen," and the student replied, "I am listening," to which the professor said, "That is the secret!"

Good conversation is like a tennis match, where we listen and respond and keep hitting back to each other, with everyone participating.

Becoming a good listener will not only make you a better and more selfless person, it will make others like you more and know you are giving them your full attention, which is becoming more and more rare.

I think we now know why God created people with two ears and one mouth, and that tells us why we should listen more before we speak. Only through real listening do we become wiser and more knowledgeable, as well as saving ourselves a lot of pain and heartache.

Forgive

Forgiveness wipes the bad thoughts and memories

*Forgiveness allows you to clear
your conscience really fast*

Unforgiveness weighs tonnes

Forgiveness sets us free

If we are to live a life that is not held back by envy, anger, jealousy, shame and regret, we must learn to forgive both ourselves and others.

Forgiveness is not only good for others but is of even greater benefit to ourselves, when we can often be far harder and more critical of ourselves than others for our past failures, regrets and mistakes.

The ancient prophets, religions and philosophers have all talked about forgiveness, and there is good reason why. We are all made imperfect. The art of forgiveness is a necessity if we are to live our best life and become a greater soul, despite the many challenges and mishaps along our journey in life.

Sadly, we see a world today that can be cruel, unfriendly and unforgiving, aside from our own sins and mistakes that we fail to recognise and thus show a lack of empathy, compassion and love towards others.

Forgiveness is designed for both ourselves and others, and only by forgiving can we live a higher and deeper, more meaningful life. Forgiveness sets us free; it plucks the roots or weeds that become wedged in our mind, such as shame, regret, anger and other negative emotions, and allows us to live life to the max as we are designed to.

Rather than forgive ourselves and others, many people live for years in a mental state of unforgiveness, anger and bitterness, all anchors to our happiness which slowly destroy us from within, bit by bit.

To free ourselves, we must forgive others, no matter what they have done to us, and we must also forgive ourselves for our mistakes and failures.

By doing this, we wipe the diseases of the mind from our memory, and strangely, we feel more relaxed and happy. The load off our shoulders vanishes immediately. One could say forgiveness is almost miracle-like in its ability to heal and renew an individual's mind.

Forgiveness is one of the greatest powers that we should practise on a regular basis. Its mental, emotional, physical and spiritual benefits cannot be paid with money, and its rewards are incredible to both ourselves and others.

Friendships

Friendship is where true wealth lies

We few, we happy few, we band of brothers; for he today that sheds his blood with me, shall be my brother
- Shakespeare (Henry V Agincourt speech)

Aristotle said in *Nicomachean Ethics* that there were three types of friendships in a man's life: utility based, pleasure based and character based. This assessment is as true today as it was thousands of years ago when he first spoke about this.

Utility friendships can be defined as what two people can do for one another and is seen around the world today with modern networking, which is a transactional relationship, and ends when one party can no longer add value to the relationship.

Pleasure-based relationships are friendships of a shared activity and the pursuit of fleeting pleasure and emotions which can be associated with sports, music, work, partying and other activities — a good time, or, as Aristotle described, the friendship of the young.

The last friendship that Aristotle described, and the one he defined as the best and one we should all look to cultivate, is a character-based friendship, where we just enjoy the friendship and companionship of another person in the most pure sense. You like hanging around with them and expect nothing in return; you enjoy your time with that person and like who they are. These people make you a better person, support you and you just like being in their company.

Friendship is one of the keys to a happy life and has become forgotten in the modern world, as people's friendships shrink in the digital age with more screen time, as loneliness rises. It's one where I have had many failures with letting great friendships rust and not making enough effort, which is very common for people in recent times. We have lost the art of maintaining friendships, with Facebook accounts having hundreds and thousands of fake friends, people who are called friends, yet we never spend time with them.

Cultivating and maintaining friendships has become harder than ever in the digital era, but we should make the effort. We will be rewarded handsomely.

Women are definitely better than men at maintaining friendships. I have learned that we often make our best friendships through school, university and sporting or other clubs, and the majority of these types of friendships are developed in our teens and early adult life. Once we get older and these outlets are no longer possible for meeting people, it becomes far harder to make new friends. Many studies about people have proven this point.

Friendship is an art and one we all need, and the best is, as Aristotle described, the pure friendship based on character rather than pleasure or business transactions. Studies have shown that around 70% to 80% of our happiness comes from relationships, and that alone shows you just how much we need healthy relationships to live a happy life.

Maintaining old friendships and developing new ones is not easy with a changing world, but it is something we must seek out — we all need them on our journey through life. Friendships sustain and support us, and no amount of money can be as rewarding as great friendships.

Social fitness

Do you exercise your social life just like your physical life?

We all need healthy social bank accounts

Loneliness is the biggest silent killer today

We all know how it is a necessity to exercise to have good health, but it is just as important to exercise socially and ensure we have good social skills and healthy supportive relationships. By exercising socially, I mean making time to interact and engage with people, having people who we can talk with, not feeling lonely, having friendships, being able to talk to someone about anything, having someone there on a bad day to support you, being able to walk into a room and interact without knowing anyone, being able to listen without losing focus, being able to make small talk with a stranger and being able to empathise with others — these are all signs of good social fitness.

Numerous studies have confirmed that relationships have the biggest impact on a person's health and happiness, but they must be cultivated to stay in good condition, just like good health.

Robert Waldinger from Harvard came up with the term "social fitness," and I believe it's a great way to review the bank account or fitness of our social life and ensure we maintain healthy social dynamics in our lives.

Just like with our physical fitness, we often don't feel like walking, running, going to the gym, joining a club or playing sport, and it is the same with our social fitness, where we don't want to make an effort to meet new friends, socialise with others or keep in touch with old friends.

But just like how our health must be maintained with good health practices daily to remain healthy, so must our social fitness be maintained, and in the digital era, this has plummeted for lots of people around the world.

Loneliness has exploded all over the world, and, sadly, many people don't have any friends today. Making friends is becoming even harder in the information age where many of us don't even interact with people at work or attend a physical worksite. Building relationships and meeting people used to be an automatic part of life but those rules no longer apply and we have to work much harder to maintain social fitness, and this requires dedicated effort.

Just like our physical fitness, if we don't use it, we lose it, and the same applies to our social fitness. If we don't maintain relationships or make an effort to engage in meeting new people, we lose it and our interpersonal skills decline, which is the same as atrophy in the physical realm.

Social fitness

Loneliness is the biggest silent killer across society today and often this is no one's fault but is a result of the modern world we now inhabit. I know how hard it can be to make new friends, especially if you have moved to many places like I have and not known a single soul.

So, attend to your social fitness by making an effort for small talk at the checkout or with the barista, strike up a conversation with a stranger, say yes to more after work drinks or other invitations and events, join clubs and groups that interest you and stay in touch with old friends.

Social fitness is hard work, just like physical fitness, but the rewards will be well worth it and you will feel so much better for making the effort to socialise more and become an even greater person. In the process, you will feel, may I say it, more human.

Hobbies

A hobby a day keeps the doldrums away
- Phyllis McGinty

Hobbies are great distractions from the worries and troubles that plague daily living
- Bill Malone

What hobbies a person has is one of the best ways to really get to know the inner workings of a person's soul. The hobbies they spend their time on and do in their spare time for no financial gain tells you a lot about them.

Hobbies and exploring passions that we enjoy give us energy, and we should explore them to the max. So many things can take energy from us, such as phones, computers, social media and toxic relationships, but our hobbies have the ability to provide a great creative and community outlet and are interests we should explore to our dying days, making us feel good in the process.

People who regularly spend time on their hobbies are happier people and have a much more grounded life. I think when we explore our hobbies, we become who we are, as Nietzsche urged us to become. Hobbies really are the inner workings of the soul and who we are.

I have many hobbies, from music, playing guitar, sport, rugby league, exercise, hiking, fishing, reading, economics, squash, travelling, and hunting, and they have always added great value to my life.

No matter what your hobby or interest is, from gardening, trains, planes, community groups, knitting, painting, photography, woodwork, dancing, cooking, hunting, or chess, follow these and they will provide a great return to your life.

Exploring our hobbies with no one around is each of us being as authentic as possible. It's good for the soul and the mind!

We need others

No man is an island
- John Donne

We all need others and that's ok

The power of leverage

It's ok if you can make me be greater

During our journey of life, we need the help and support of others and we should not be embarrassed to seek this out. In fact, if we don't get the assistance of others, we are likely to pay a huge price and be at a great disadvantage.

The Bible talks about when two or three are together, nothing is impossible when they are in perfect unity. Another way of looking at this is that the power of leverage multiplies exponentially when a group of people are working in perfect harmony with the same goal in mind, compared to one person on their own trying to do it all.

History has proven the power of groups and teamwork with modern inventions, new businesses, successful marriages, and families, military battles, boards with excellent governance and many other examples.

I think of how some of my favourite musicians such as Bruce Springsteen, Neil Young, Bob Dylan and many others go to new levels when playing with their backing bands, such as the E Street Band, and Crazy Horse for Bruce Springsteen and Neil Young as examples. Eddie Vedder is a great solo singer but his best music has always been with Pearl Jam. These are all great artists but others lift them higher.

The talented boxer meets an experienced trainer who takes the boxer to new levels with education, training and physical and mental preparation. The husband and wife who can complement each other with masculine and feminine traits make each other greater and thus have a closer bond.

No one has ever achieved anything of real substance without the support of others. Even solo performers and professionals always have support from someone.

There is a certain synergistic energy that sometimes can't be explained with groups, and it can take individuals to completely new levels when they mix their talents with others in perfect unity.

Ego is one reason why we don't seek out the support of others, when we should humble ourselves and ask for help. It's okay to ask for help and support and admit that others can make us become greater.

None of us has all the answers, and we all have our strengths and weaknesses. School teaches students to compete rather than cooperate and tap into the power of leverage and synergistic energy of a group working together. Rather than teaching about teamwork and unity, they teach a curriculum that focuses on who gets the highest score on their grades and being an individual, when the real world rewards and cares about teamwork and unity rather than grades and beating others.

Seek out support and find those who can help you on your journey. They will lift you up and make you greater.

Helping others

Everybody needs someone

Give and you shall receive
- Bible (Luke 6:38)

We can never truly live a great life without enriching the lives of others, and I believe it is our duty and responsibility that we give back and help others during our lives.

Look at how many people have helped us during our lifetimes! The support really is incalculable when we take some time to reflect on the assistance we have received from birth.

Teachers, volunteers, educators, friends, family, clubs and various other services have all given to us for nothing and it is a responsibility and duty that we also pass the tradition on to the next generation. Look at what the hands of others have built that we each take for granted and use every day, from roads, hospitals, cars, planes, trains, computers, and recipes. What we have received from others really is infinite and incalculable.

We can help others in many ways and it is true that the more we grow and become, the more is expected in return for what has been given to us.

We can give of our time, money, talents, hearts and souls, intellect, spirit, and love for life. There is no end to what we can give, but give we must!

The world can be a cruel and lonely place, and if we have been given much and not just in monetary terms, we should give back and serve and support our fellow humans.

This can be a kind word of support, a donation to a charity whose cause you support, really listening to someone who has gone through an emotionally tough time, touching a person with a book, poem or kind word, helping people set goals and achieve their dreams, identifying with others from your own painful experiences, making the kids laugh, and helping your inner circle, from your wife and children to close friends and community members.

Giving makes us healthier and happier and we can never become a fully developed individual without learning the graces of giving. Let's pay our rent to the world the way it was meant to be paid.

Association

Association is subtle in its effects
- Jim Rohn

While we most definitely need the support and help of others in life, as discussed in a previous chapter, we must also ensure we associate with those who can lift us up, and limit or stop the negative influence of others who can drag us down.

The people we hang around with play a massive role in influencing our lives, and so often that influence of association is both so subtle and gradual that we don't notice it, for positive or negative.

If you hang around a person who exercises, fair chance you will begin to exercise; if you hang around readers who discuss books, fair chance you will start reading books; if you hang around people who like to travel, fair chance you will want to travel. We see this in the workplace, where the smokers often hang out together for regular cigarette breaks, the gossipers love to chat about everything and anything, and people who love reality television love to talk with people who watch similar shows.

Jim Rohn said there were three categories when associating with others that we need to examine, and he said we should place them into three groups, called expanded association, limited association, and dissociation.

After some time of reflection, you may recognize that you need to cut some weeds out of your life and disassociate with some people who are not good influences for you. Whilst this is never easy, it is necessary if you are to remove those from your life who are negative and are dragging you down the wrong road.

Some relationships we can't completely break, such as with family, friendships, and work and business colleagues, but we can limit the amount of time we have with these people. This is often hard, but is required if we are to stay on our path and not get knocked off track. I have had family members and work colleagues in the past who I have had to limit my association with, as I realised their influence was negative in my life.

The last one is expanded association; this is spending time with others who make us better people, who have strong ethics, have passion for life, are generous and are stimulating and can hold a great conversation, and you just enjoy being in their company. These people's influence can have a huge impact on us, and we should always seek people of such ilk who can add great value to our lives.

Chase people's needs, not your wants

*Ask not what your country can do for you –
ask what you can do for your country*
- John Kennedy

If you ask any person what they want in life, they will likely reply with such common responses as: better health, more money, a big house, a flash car, a better relationship or a variety of other wants and needs.

Most businesses are started with the goal of earning more money, to be your own boss or to get out of the rat race. This is all well and good, but there is one major problem with this attitude and philosophy. By chasing our own desires, we can't get rich!

John Kennedy was on the money when he urged Americans to "Ask not what your country can do for you — ask what you can do for your country." To be of service!

Many individuals and businesses fall into the trap of thinking only about their own desires and wants, and forget one of the key ingredients to success. Unless we shift our focus onto other people's needs and wants and become of more service as Kennedy implored Americans to do, we can never get what we seek.

To do this, we must pursue other people's needs and forget our wants. It's counterintuitive, but by focusing on others' needs, we generally get what we want.

Zig Ziglar said it best: "If you help people get what they want, you can have everything you want."

Luckily for us, people all around the world have great needs and wants, from great food, travel, services of all kinds, entertainment, transportation, housing, finances, knowledge, support and health. The needs of others are endless, and by taking some time to see what others want and desire, we can then work out how we can help them and get everything we want.

Chase others' needs, not your own, and you can't help but enrich your life and those of others in the process.

Responsibility and duty

If it is to be, it is up to me
- William H Johnsen

Responsibility is the mark of a great leader

I slept and I dreamt that life was joy. I awoke and I saw that life was duty. I worked - and behold, duty was joy
- Rabindranath Tagore

Two of the most important words I think you should really reflect upon and build as a foundation to your life are "duty" and "responsibility." These are not merely words but characteristics that have stood the test of time and are the mark of real maturity and growth.

If a person bases their life on these, there's a fair chance they will live a great and honourable life, one that has the respect of their peers and true confidence from within.

Take charge and responsibility for your life, because no one is coming to save you. No one's going to help you with your health, finances, career, relationships, hobbies, lifestyle, knowledge, and other habits. I learned this the hard way when no one came to save me from my difficulties, and I quickly found out: if it was to be, it was up to me to change my lot.

Duty is one of the most beautiful words in the English language and epitomises a life well lived in deed and service. As I have gotten older, I can see why so many past figures have talked about duty.

Joy and fulfilment can only come from duty, that is, doing the work that must be done and what life is asking us to do. Sometimes it expects the impossible and the dangerous.

It's your duty to live a great life, to take responsibility for what your plot is and possibly others outside your care, even if some of it was not your fault, or life is asking you to take on challenges that seem insurmountable. If we cultivate and develop both responsibility and duty, we are reaching the highest levels of maturity, and, in the process, finding real joy and honour.

Suffering

Suffering occurs when expectation meets reality

A lot of our own suffering comes from unrealistic expectations or having a rigid state of mind on certain outcomes in our life.

One of the quickest ways to suffer and experience pain and anger is when our expectations collide with reality. The hope of a new job, a new relationship, financial freedom, weight loss, adventures, and many other hopes and desires can quickly lead to pain when the outcome does not go as planned or as we had hoped or expected.

We have all had our fair share of pain and disappointment, and experienced those events when things we had hoped for don't go to plan and the pain of reality comes crashing down on our hopes.

To free ourselves of this pain, we need to free our mind from those expectations that often lead to suffering, pain and pressure, holding us back from happiness and joy.

Having set thoughts on how something should turn out is a quick way to unhappiness, as we cannot control events outside of our control. It's all well and good having high expectations, but we must also deal with the consequences when those high hopes do not come to fruition.

To do this, we must release and remove those rigid thoughts or set outcomes and unrealistic expectations that only cause pain and frustration. We must have no expectations, and free ourselves from a mindset that is anchored to a set outcome.

The minute we free ourselves from set outcomes and certain thoughts, we take the world off our shoulders. We don't let outside events and outcomes control our happiness, as we have freed our thoughts from set outcomes and replaced those with a happy outcome, no matter what happens.

We don't meet that right person, we don't get that promotion, we don't get picked for the team, we don't get that bonus are all examples of where we need to control our expectations and response to outcomes which often we have no control over.

One of the hardest things to manage in our lives is our own expectations. Some of the greatest writers and thinkers throughout history have said to go forward with a positive expectation that what you desire shall come, and others, such as Buddhists, believe that suffering occurs when expectation meets reality and we should limit our expectations to reduce future disappointment and pain.

I have struggled with this balance, and, like many, have been disappointed when my own expectations have collided with

Suffering

reality and I have not obtained what I had once hoped for. It can be very emotionally draining.

We live in a world where advertising and keeping up with the Joneses is shoved down our throats relentlessly. We are told to believe that if we don't have the latest gadgets or this type of lifestyle or relationship, we are inferior and missing out, when really, it is all a grab for our money.

The best option to become free from this trap is to live life without expectations. Don't have a structured mindset on how it all must unfold. We can only control ourselves. We can't control outside forces and we must free ourselves from attachment to certain outcomes.

This will free us and our minds and take a great load off our shoulders in the process.

Find meaning and purpose

What is your why?

The how gets easier when the why is strong
- Frederich Nietzsche

He who has a why to live can bear any how
- Frederich Nietzsche

Our default position to a successful life in terms of the world's view is often measured in monetary terms alone, but we have all read and heard the stories of many millionaires and billionaires on how empty they felt — despite all the money in the world, they were still miserable inside and never found happiness or true fulfilment.

The focus on wealth and material things can lead many to go down the wrong road. We often make career and family decisions based on money alone, which can leave a huge hole in our lives, and we end up sooner or later facing an existential crisis.

That existential crisis has now become rampant globally: our lives have little or no meaning, with no purpose, and, as a result, we see depression and mental health disorders at

Find meaning and purpose

record levels and growing higher every year, particularly in some of the richest countries in the world.

Victor Frankl, who was once a prisoner of war in a Nazi prison camp, is maybe best qualified on how to find meaning and purpose in one's life. He wrote one of the best books of all time on the subject called *Man's Search for Meaning*, from his experiences in prison.

Frankl, who was a psychiatrist before entering prison, would go on to create a new form of therapy called logotherapy, which was all about finding meaning and purpose for one's life.

He said there were three ways of finding meaning and purpose in one's life:

- Work - Doing something significant
- Love - Caring for another person
- Dignity in suffering - Giving our suffering meaning

Frankl said the love for his wife, to see her again, and to finish his book, and work from his experiences in prison on logotherapy gave him strong enough reasons to want to survive the prison camp and live. He said those who did not have a strong enough why or reasons to live were the one who died the quickest in camp.

When released from prison, Frankl devoted his life to helping people find meaning and purpose in their lives, and is still admired by millions for his gifts to humanity from that terrible experience in a Nazi prison.

Meaning and purpose has become quite a common theme, with many TED talk-like shows, but even they can misinterpret this subject.

Meaning and purpose give our life substance and depth and the reason to get up out of bed every day with great drive and determination.

Meaning and purpose can be the fuel that drives our engine, but often we don't have this. Instead, we find ourselves drifting along aimlessly.

Meaning and purpose is within reach for all of us if we take the time to look at who we are and how we can best use our talents and abilities, and how we can serve the greater good with what we have, and determine what is most important in our lives.

Sometimes we confuse our passions with finding our meaning. This can lead to the hobbies that we once loved becoming a chore and unenjoyable when monetary returns fail to materialise.

We can find our meaning and purpose in many ways and Frankl's advice above is a great starting point. One of the best ways is to find a great cause that stirs our hearts.

What is it that the world wants me to do or is there a problem that only I can solve that can help the world? I wrote my first book about rugby league and about the many issues plaguing the game that I didn't think were getting discussed enough by leaders and media representatives in the sport, and since no

Find meaning and purpose

one would talk about it, I wrote the book myself. It was that cause which drove me to finish the book.

Our purpose can free us from the 9-5 routine, enable us to find financial independence and give us more control of our destiny, to travel and spend more time with our families or to solve a diverse range of problems that the world needs solutions to.

Only very few individuals find their meaning and purpose at a very young age. For most of us, it's a long road via cumulative experiences of both a positive and negative nature, for us to eventually find our true calling or find meaning in suffering or in our relationships.

Earl Nightingale said there were two kinds of people: river people and goal oriented people. He said river people come into life knowing from a young age exactly what they want to do for their entire life. This can be seen with people who love art, music, animals, or science and would love to be doing nothing else. For the majority, though, finding our passion and meaning is a long race and we are more likely to be goal people, who never find one river that satisfies our life, but we have many goals that give us direction and drive.

Only by taking the time to really know ourselves, our talents and how we can best serve the world we live in can we truly find our meaning and purpose in life, whether we are goal oriented or we are river people. Give yourself time and let it unfold without putting undue pressure on yourself.

Numbers and likes

Social media is more dangerous than drugs, booze, gambling and all the other bad habits we develop combined

With the invention of social media and other technology, we have seen social behaviour change drastically in ways no one could have expected or anticipated before the information age.

One of the tragedies of these modern inventions is seeing the change across society, with many people now becoming addicted to technology and seeking influence and attention with selfish motives.

Many folks — and not just teens or young adults — are doing all sorts of silly things to get attention, with the dopamine thrill of numbers and likes creating a society that has no real foundation or real community spirit, compared to prior generations.

You see it relentlessly across social media platforms, with everyone trying to outdo one another with new pics, the perfect relationship, travel adventures, new cars, houses and other toys, all aimed at likes and numbers to impress.

This trend has made society so much more shallow, one where the quality things in life are ignored and replaced with sensation, drama, noise, grandstanding and other ugly behaviours.

The seeking of numbers, hits and likes really shows the lack of self esteem many around the world have today, where that calm individual who is comfortable in their own skin and does not need the applause and acknowledgement of others is becoming rarer and rarer.

It's not what we get, but what we become that matters — who we really are — and, sadly, many are doing ridiculous things to be noticed and gain attention.

Real self esteem, confidence and authenticity is knowing who we are and not needing the likes or applause of others. It's being able to go against the crowd and stay true to yourself and be confident and comfortable with who you are.

The search for numbers and likes is literally killing Western society, with a phone or other electronic device always in someone's hand or lap, and people unable to engage in proper conversation and having little ability to concentrate. Many people today cannot have a face-to-face conversation without feeling uncomfortable.

Study after study is now proving the dangers with social media and it is something we should take note of if we are to stay sane and remain authentic happy individuals who do not move to the push and pull of modern society.

Forget chasing likes and numbers — our foundation must be built much deeper than this plastic digital culture. Instead, we should know who we are and have self respect for ourselves, and not become like others who will do anything for the attention and applause of the crowd. Be the private person who doesn't need likes and hits, who knows who they are and what they want from life, and who doesn't need to flaunt things in everyone's face.

That's the real mark of a mature and authentic person that we should aim for, one that has deep roots and is not moved by the new fads and trends of the day.

Stimulation can drive you

*Stimulation comes from the outside,
determination comes from within*

There will be many times in your life when you will feel flat and lack the desire and energy to pursue your goals or keep up with your daily disciplines, when routine can become a hard slog. The solution to maintaining high levels of motivation and discipline is to continually seek out stimulation that can refuel your motor and drive you forward, no matter how hard things may be at present.

Stimulation can come in many forms: from books, CDs, podcasts, movies, music, conversation, and experiences from both good and bad, and we should use all these forms and sources to help us throughout life.

Personal development legend Napoleon Hill talked about how many great men from history rose to great heights via the stimulation of the right women and influence. He gave some excellent examples, including the life of French leader Napoleon Bonaparte, who rose to incredible heights, but when he got rid of his long-time partner Joséphine, he quickly fell from such heights. Hill also mentioned how Abraham Lincoln was heavily influenced and inspired by his stepmother in his early years and that this relationship would drive his ambition and determination, despite enormous struggles and setbacks, to become the American president.

Stimulation in many forms not only provides energy and fuel, it also gives us awareness, understanding and ideas. The ideas from books have changed countless lives: from losing weight and becoming healthy, becoming financially independent, improving relationships, learning skills, learning history and much, much more. In fact, I would argue that unless you have the stimulation, you cannot change!

As I have mentioned in an earlier chapter, the reason I achieved so little in my twenties was: (1) I was not stimulated, (2) I didn't have the vehicle for achievement, and (3) I didn't know how to change and grow. These are all great points on how you can't change when you don't have the knowledge, skills or vehicle to move in a new direction.

The gaining of knowledge and stimulation opens all sorts of wonderful opportunities for our lives, but if we don't seek them out, we become less and less, and eventually start going backwards.

Just like a car needing fuel or a body needing food, our minds and spirits need regular stimulation from a variety of sources and inputs. We must seek it out always!

Focus on the process, not the event

It's a process
- Moneyball (Brad Pitt)

The score will take care of itself
- Bill Walsh

If you watch any Hollywood movie, they will normally give you the shortened version of the script and go straight to events and significant moments in the storyline, as they try to build drama in the story whilst running within a compressed set timeline for viewers.

This Hollywood-like scenario has now made many in society ill disciplined and impatient with their own goals and desires, and believe life is like a movie. Nothing could be further from the truth! Many now focus on events which are what people only see in the movies and social media feeds, and totally forget the most important part, the actual process to any achievement that leads to the end or achievement of a major event.

There can be no major completion of a goal without a process, and processes are not easy or sexy. There is a reason why

Hollywood leaves these out of movies and only shows you the exciting parts and major events.

Process takes time and is often a hard grind, with many ups and downs along the road. It can take many years to achieve a goal and sometimes even many decades.

The world has the microwave attitude of quick success, but all journeys are a process. We should forget the outcomes and become more focused on the process, or, as former San Francisco 49's coach Bill Walsh advised, "The score will take care of itself."

The process is nothing more than what we do on a daily and weekly basis. It is the steps to achieving our goals, the hard work, planning and discipline side of things. As Jim Rohn so eloquently and simply said, "Discipline is the bridge between goals and accomplishment."

What are the processes? They are those key daily disciplines you need to apply to achieve the health you want, the books you need to read to become wise, the finances you desire, the relationships you hope for, the adventures you seek, and the life you dream about.

These are not merely pipe dreams but are attainable with hard work, belief, discipline, and going through a rigorous process to reach our goals and dreams. Forget the end result and become more concerned with the process and doing each day as best as you can.

Motivation over enforced discipline

What looks like self discipline to many is actually real enjoyment and fun

Find the habits that best suit you

Don't rely on willpower or self control

Much has been written about discipline and self control and its importance in one's life, but numerous new studies are now confirming how discipline and self control have been confused and misrepresented. The need for willpower for a disciplined life is actually far less relied upon than we think, and can often be confused with enjoyment and motivation.

We all know the person who loses an enormous amount of weight only to put this weight back on in due time. They had starved themselves and exercised religiously to lose the weight, only to fall back into those bad habits through lack of willpower and self control, and slowly go back to their old ways.

A key point we must become aware of is: What many people think is discipline is not really discipline but is actual enjoyment of an activity that they are motivated to perform, for those who have certain habits they enjoy. Many elite swimmers get up at 4am to do hours of laps in the pool, and what most people would think is hell, is not hell or even discipline, but enjoyment to those swimmers. They actually enjoy swimming and doing lap after lap in the early hours of the morning while most are sleeping. This does not feel like discipline to them. For you or me, who don't enjoy swimming or getting up at 4am, we would think this is absolute hell and not fun at all if we were forced to do this every day. But for those swimmers, it is enjoyment, and they are motivated to perform this activity.

We don't realise that those people who live on salads and fat-free or sugar-free foods actually enjoy many of those foods, rather than using self control and willpower, as we are led to believe. In James Clear's best-selling book *Atomic Habits*, he stated: Those that develop excellent habits set up the environment to support themselves and use cues and routines to help with their habits, rather than rely on self control and willpower.

We have seen a wave of fitness gurus in recent years urging people to do all sorts of strenuous activities to get fit, strong and healthy, from crossfit, powerlifting, Zumba, and other extreme physical activities, and what often gets missed in the message is that those fitness gurus actually enjoy performing those sorts of high intense activities and it does not feel like discipline to them. They don't need extra motivation, just like the early morning swimmers. What is fun to them and the swimmers may not be the same for other individuals. For most others, it will require extra willpower and self control to perform and will likely result in those people falling down with motivation and discipline issues when forced to perform, as they don't enjoy performing those activities.

New studies are showing that self control is overrated and our willpower is quite weak over the long haul. Instead, the key to discipline and self control may be in finding alignment between our natural motivation and the things we like to do.

I love to walk, go to the gym and play squash to stay active, and they require discipline to perform, but they don't feel like discipline to me, as I am motivated to perform these activities and never have motivational struggles to start them. If you asked a regular group of squash players at your local club, they would not say it is a discipline or feels like one but something they enjoy playing very much and are motivated to perform on a regular basis, and they find it easy to keep up a regular playing schedule.

Maybe then, the key to discipline and self control is: rather than forcing ourselves to do something we don't like or enjoy, to find natural motivation and enjoyment through activities that we love to do.

Winston Churchill's life is a perfect example; he would stay up to 2am, 3am or even 4am most nights, get up at 8am and then have a two-hour nap at 3pm the next day. He would be ridiculed in today's society, but Churchill's routine worked perfectly for him, with an early and late creative shift that would result in him writing 44 praised books and leading England through World War Two.

If you don't like the gym or swimming but love tennis, then play tennis for your fitness. If you don't like investing in real estate but love commodities, then invest in precious metals. If you hate salads, then find a diet that does not include salads and suits the foods you like. If you like sleeping in late rather than being an early riser, then train at night rather than first thing in the morning and enjoy your sleep-ins. If you like reading sports books over classic novels, then read sports books. If you like romantic novels over non-fiction, then read romantic novels. The key is to find the habit that best suits you and your own personal interests, and to cultivate this.

Find the activities that you like and enjoy, and this will require far less willpower and self control from you, and you will be on your way to both motivation and discipline and a path that is much easier and uniquely yours and one you are likely to keep over a lifetime.

Everything is energy

E = mc²
- Albert Einstein

Where awareness goes, energy flows
- Dandapani

There has been incredible progress made in recent decades in the realm of quantum mechanics, which is basically how the world operates on the smallest scale. It is mind-blowing how the world operates and much more is still to be understood, but what is known can also provide an incredible insight on how to live and find success.

Quantum mechanics has confirmed that everything in the world is energy, and without this energy, nothing would exist. We live in a closed universe, and energy can change forms but it can't escape the universe. You see this in everyday life, from a burning fire changing form, the skyline moving from clear sky to thunderstorm back to clear skyline, and grass growing in the summer then dying in the winter. Energy is always transmuting into other forms.

Everything that moves or has life has a certain amount of energy attached to it. Energy is one of the great mysteries of the world and is becoming instrumental in understanding the human race and our nature.

If you don't believe everything is energy, here is a quick test. Have you ever been close to someone who is really mad? When they were mad, could you feel their anger and energy vibrate? Of course you could! This is the energy radiating off them and the vibrations that you are picking up and feeling.

Without energy, nothing in this world would exist! The greatest energy we release comes from our own desires. Desire unlocks energy, and it can be a tremendous advantage when utilised and channelled in the right way.

Have you ever seen a couple in love for the first time? The energy they possess is incredible. They can drive for days, not sleep, and still possess incredible energy, and this all flows from the passionate desire they have for their new partner. You see this passion and energy radiate from people who love doing the work they love, from musicians, artists, writers, and sport stars who have incredible passion and drive for their craft.

Sadly, the energy of the past is one of the greatest hindrances to us reaching our full potential. So many are held back by the failures and fears of the past, which act like an anchor on our ship of progress. As explained, without energy, nothing exists, and our minds are also energy and can carry the negative fears and failures of the past that hold us back from the life we desire.

If we are to break the chains of the past, we must work with energy and not against it. As everything is energy and we live in a closed universe, we must create greater energy from new experiences that remove the bad memories and failures of the past that make us weak. Greater energy eliminates lesser energy, and, as we work with universal laws, it will change the form in our minds like it does with the burning fire, changing weather patterns and grass growing and dying examples. Our negative memories of the past can be wiped out with new experiences that bring in new and greater energy forms.

Replace the failed past relationships with new relationships, past fears and failures with new successes that wipe out the past, past inactivity with intelligent activity, image problems with new images that boost our self esteem, and utilise desire to harness energy to our advantage. This is one of the greatest new discoveries in personal growth.

Learning to understand how energy plays a vital role in our lives, we can pluck the weeds from the past and rewire our minds with new thoughts and experiences. This leads to new energy that creates success and wipes the past memories away that hold so many of us back.

Mental paradigms

It takes repetition to change your paradigm

Your paradigm is created by association, media, school, and past failures, and most people have no clue

We often go through life not realising what is holding us back, and often that anchor is what is going on between our ears. Our wonderful minds are an incredible instrument, unlimited with possibilities. I realised one day that I never have been provided with any training on how to use or develop this great power that often lies dormant. School never taught me about it, modern culture rarely discusses it, and instead, bombards our minds with endless trash that makes us dumber or overloaded with information. Workplaces provide little or no training and development on using our minds. They tell us what to think but not how to think.

Bob Proctor was one of the first teachers to talk about mental paradigms. He believed that our paradigm determines what happens in our life, and, unfortunately, most people have been hijacked by their own paradigms, without any awareness of this. Proctor said the past events, past failures, lack of awareness, poor education, the modern culture of fear and

Mental paradigms

other negative emotions have all played a role in undermining our wonderful minds. The paradigm, to Proctor, was a mental programme that was deep inside our subconscious minds. When you look at the inputs that go into our minds on a constant basis, you can see why so many people are not happier or achieving more. Non-stop negative news, thinking on past failures, bad associations, and limited beliefs are all too common.

To repair and remodel our paradigm is not an easy task, if one has been subjected to many years of negativity and fear and constant bombardment from many other sources. But being aware that we can change our paradigm, and with persistence, it is totally possible to do so and to change our lives in the process.

To change our paradigm, we need to start feeding our mind relentlessly with good information, understanding why we have not gotten what we desire in life, and associate with people who lift us up and inspire us to be the best we can be.

Just by becoming aware of our paradigm and how it can be positive or negative is a huge step. Make no mistake: if you're trying to change your life, your old paradigms will do all that is possible to hold you back.

Changing your paradigm will be one of the hardest challenges you will ever face. When you decide to go down a different road or chase a new big goal, the ghosts and fears of the past will try to stop you and drag you down at every chance. We must know this is natural and proceed nonetheless. Those scary new ideals and changes of starting a business, taking a chance on love, travelling to remote locations for work, investing money, or changing careers will be tough, as you fight the old paradigm that wants to drag you back.

All change starts from within, and the centrepiece of this is our own thinking and paradigms, which are deep-rooted in our subconscious minds. Let's start cultivating the life we want and remove those barriers and negative thoughts that kill our dreams and hopes. This is done through awareness, education and the continual process of pushing new ideas to form a new paradigm in our subconscious mind.

The world we look for

We become what we think about
- Earl Nightingale

Henry David Thoreau said many an object is not seen because, although it comes within the range of our visual ray, it does not come within the range of our intellectual ray, in other words, because we are not looking for it.

Show any two people the same picture and each will see it differently. One man sees a plot of land, another sees a new motel or development. That is the power of the world we look for and the results both positive or negative, though slight, can be incredible.

Many people today are consumed by fear, worry and doubts and can't seem to see anything beyond their own worries and fears. If we are to live how we were made by our creator, we need to remove those deadly emotions and cultivate the world and life we seek for ourselves.

We find the world we look for and we must open our minds to the opportunities that are around each of us, no matter what our story is.

There are miracles and unlimited opportunity all around us, but it takes effort to go deep within our souls and find the world we look for. We need courage and clear thinking to find the world and life we seek.

The pursuit of happiness can only come from the happiness of pursuit

There is a time in every man's education when he arrives at the conviction that envy is ignorance; that imitation is suicide; that he must take himself for better, for worse, as his portion; that though the wide universe is full of good, no kernel of nourishing corn can come to him but through his toil bestowed on that plot of ground which is given to him to till
- Ralph Waldo Emerson

A man should learn to detect and watch that gleam of light which flashes across his mind from within, more than the lustre of the firmament of bards and sages. Yet he dismisses without notice his thought, because it is his
- Ralph Waldo Emerson

Those only are happy (I thought) who have their minds fixed on some object other than their own happiness; on the happiness of others, on the improvement of mankind, even on some art or pursuit, followed not as a means, but as itself an ideal end. Aiming thus at something else, they find happiness by the way
- John Stuart Mill

*Life itself is the greatest gift of all and
yet many pay no attention to this*

Happiness is in the doing, not the results

*One of the major regrets of the elderly on their
deathbed is: I waited too long to start living*

Over the last few decades, we have seen a wave of teachers, gurus, new age types, YouTubers, writers and other salespeople all promise and attempt to sell the secret to happiness. They all sell happiness like it is some magic pill. Nothing could be further from the truth as millions get conned in a giant scam and eventually find out just how elusive happiness really can be.

There is no magic pill, as many have learned, and going directly after something like happiness will result in happiness eluding you, like chasing a butterfly. Many people never find true happiness when they attempt to go directly to the source.

Happiness is not an end in itself or a result of having money, possessions, status or other external events, and can only be found from within by forgetting ourselves and using our time well to develop ourselves fully, having a true cause that makes us feel alive and in serving and helping others on their journey.

The pursuit of happiness can only come from the happiness of pursuit

We find true joy, peace, contentment and happiness in the pursuit, not the end outcome, and this is a key point that so many people forget or don't know. Happiness is a byproduct of our actions, and by forgetting ourselves in work, finding meaningful causes or helping others, in the process, we can find true joy and contentment with our thoughts, feelings and actions.

The least happy people are usually self centred, selfish, and only concerned about themselves and focused on what they are getting rather than giving, and have created an island of their selfish worries around them. Sadly, this has become all too common around the world.

We are responsible for what we think, feel and do, and so it is the same with our own happiness.

I have found that when I do work of any type: writing, creating music, reading, adding value in business for colleagues and clients, exercising, playing sport or helping others, I feel energised afterwards and so much better, and radiate inner pride and personal satisfaction. The same can happen with you with your own interests, hobbies, work and relationships.

Peace, joy, pride, and contentment are all byproducts of your character in action, relentlessly pursuing your goals and desires, having an adventurous life, working on your character, finding your true cause that stirs deep emotion within your heart, building meaningful personal relationships, using your talents to develop yourself fully and serving and helping others, and, strangely, in the process, you take your mind off yourself and feel abundant positive energy. This is where real joy comes from, not when you are wrapped up in yourself. It never comes when you chase it directly — it eludes you, like so many have found out.

Happiness is in the pursuit and not the means of an end. We need to be reminded of this often.

Total commitment

I ain't gonna quit

They can kill me but they can't eat me
- HillBilly saying

*Total commitment is nothing more
than faith expressed in action*
- William E Bailey

Faith without works is dead
- The Bible (James 2:14)

In any endeavour, persistence is often the difference between success or failure. Persistence is not easy, and separates the men from the boys, showing through their actions whether they are really committed to their goals and dreams or it's just talk.

Persistence is an absolute necessity in any endeavour, and without it, failure is certain. People who may lack the skills or knowledge can often outachieve others with more natural talent through nothing more than persistence and hard work.

Total commitment is nothing more than a state of mind that no matter what happens or what adversity you face, you are going to achieve what you set out to do. It's a firm decision that you are going all-in for what you want. It's cutting the rope and not going back to the safety of the dock harbour. It's an all-in decision and there is no going back. You are totally committed to what you have chosen to go after.

Persistence, or total commitment, as I call it, is a state of mind and is shown through my decisions, actions and focus, that what I have set out to achieve I will achieve, no matter what I face. No matter if it rains, snows, is extremely windy, cold or hot, I am committed to achieving this. I ain't gonna quit, no matter what comes my way. I am totally committed!

If you bring the attitude of total commitment to what you do, it offers many other benefits, including taking the pressure off achieving any goal, as you have now made a firm decision that no matter what comes, you will climb the mountain. There is no turning back and you can now give your goal totality of focus. With a total commitment attitude, you can now focus on improving skills and knowledge, knowing that you have the right mindset and attitude, and are open to improvement and mentorship along the way.

Total commitment is necessary to achieve any goal and separates the winners from the losers, the talkers from the doers. Total commitment is an attribute that can be developed and is often the difference between success and failure, and why the less talented person passes the more talented rival.

Meeting the right partner

When you look up and see her, will you be ready?

Love is a battlefield
- Doc Love

Bottom-line factor - Only a woman's actions truly reflect her feelings toward you
- Doc Love

Interest level cuts through everything
- Doc Love

One of the biggest decisions in any person's life is whether you will get married or remain single. It is such a big decision that has so much weight and influence on how our lives may turn out and the degree of our own personal happiness, and yet for a decision that is life changing, we receive virtually no training or education on it.

School and modern education teach nothing about marriage and how to select a suitable partner who will be supportive throughout one's life. Churches seem to be one of the last traditions that teach anything on the subject, but even they have slipped in recent times.

Throughout my life, I have seen the disastrous consequences of people who have chosen the wrong partner and then become tangled in messy divorces, long court cases and financial pain, unable to visit their children, with deep-rooted emotional scars that some never recover from.

Many never do their due diligence on one of life's biggest decisions, and, as a result, there are huge consequences when love turns to hate and bitterness.

Men are particularly poor at selecting the right partner, with women being at least ten years older mentally than guys when they have to give birth so young, and this dating game is their natural battlefield. Most men just focus on the woman's looks and turn a blind eye to her character and the key traits needed for a successful relationship.

Napoleon Hill said the right influence of the perfect female partner could lift men to incredible heights, and he uses examples of Napoleon Bonaparte, Winston Churchill and other leaders who rose to great heights when they met their respective partners.

Doc Love aka Tom Hodges wrote *The Dating Dictionary*, later to be called *The System*. It is considered the godfather of modern dating for men. I believe his groundbreaking material written in the 1980s still stands true today and is essential reading for any man or woman to become more attractive and to identify key traits in a partner. Doc Love interviewed an incredible ten thousand plus women across his career, asking women what they liked and disliked in men and why they stayed with one man rather than another.

Doc Love said a man must possess three key traits to attract women, these being the 3 Cs of Confidence, Control (made up of discipline, patience and self control) and Challenge. Your maintenance programme to keep the girl was respect, affection, romance and humour. Doc Love says men should not worry about their own interest level but instead focus on the interest level of the woman, before knowing whether to pursue her. Without the woman having some interest, nothing will happen, but too often, men only look at their own interest level and ego and try to force themselves on the woman and get rejected.

Challenge is perhaps the biggest missing ingredient in romance today, with many women dying for men to be a challenge and make her work to win you over.

Doc Love goes on to say the ideal partner for a man is a woman who has high interest in him and possesses a great attitude made up of integrity, honesty and loyalty, is a giver rather than a taker, and is flexible and not structured or hardheaded, and has little or no baggage or scars.

In a world that is becoming more and more polarised and is pushing division between the sexes, Doc Love's sound advice is desperately needed for many men who have little knowledge or understanding of women and want a relationship that will bring happiness and joy.

Many women around the world are desperate for men to return to their masculine roots rather than the feminine trend that has spread like wildfire. The opposite sexes are complementary and not competitors, despite what has been pushed with a new wave of feminism and Marxism in recent times.

Men projecting the traits of confidence, self control and being a challenge, plus treating their partner with respect, affection, romance and humour will be giving themselves the best chance to attract and maintain quality women in their life.

Finances

Profits are better than wages
- Jim Rohn

Financial independence is another word for freedom

Cashflow - the most important word for your finances
- Robert Kiyosaki

Debt is a chain of slavery

Rich Dad Poor Dad author Robert Kiyosaki has long advocated that students are not taught the basics of financial education at school, and this huge and deliberate omission in the education system has led to tens of millions of people around the world being chained by debts and loans and remaining financially illiterate, often resulting in living in poverty and despair as they get older.

Our whole education curriculum is absent of wise information about understanding economics and financial education, when it is one of the biggest keys to our lives and those we provide for. Without a strong financial base, we can never find freedom and security! Not having a sound financial base only leads to fear, worry, arguments, broken relationships, stress, and poor health, and we should avoid these negatives at all costs and find inner peace with a sound financial base.

Basic money education includes topics such as profit, loss, income, expenses, assets, liabilities, savings, investments, stocks, bonds, real estate, interest rates, cashflow, taxes, debts, interest, inflation, deflation, gold, silver, commodities, and Bitcoin/crypto. Entrepreneurship, business and financial studies are absent from modern education, and only through self education or mentorship will we understand and become competent with these subjects.

If we are to take full control of our lives and determine our own destiny and not be dependent on the government or others, we must make the decision to not become poor, and educate ourselves on how to become financially independent and have a sound understanding of economics and personal finance so we can provide for ourselves and others and ensure inner peace and not be controlled by outside events when tough times do come.

Without financial security we can never have freedom, and without money we are restricted from living the life of our dreams. It stops us from the travel we wish to do, the house or car we wish to purchase, helping our families out, generously giving to worthy causes we support, starting a business or retiring on our terms. These all come from a sound financial base.

One of the key lessons I have learned is that our financial rewards all the years of our lives will be in direct proportion to the service we provide. The formula is simple: the more people we serve, the more money we earn! Our rewards in life will always be in exact proportion to our contributions. This is basic 101 Finance that has become forgotten in a complex world. We must sow to reap, but today, a generation has been taught to take and take and depend on the government, and have the attitude of: What's in it for me? Governments across the globe are saturated in record levels of debt as inflation soars around the world, with millions hoping their government will provide for them in later years. It is a disaster waiting to happen and one that will leave many a person destitute and desperate in years to come and why we need to take full responsibility for our personal finances.

Money is the harvest from our production, and to get a good harvest, we must produce, invest and serve. The secret always comes back to us and what we are doing!

To create wealth, you must either be an investor or be in business. The tax system favours these investment instruments, whilst employees are taxed the highest. Most rich people throughout history are investors, business owners or both, and success does indeed leave clues.

Build, work, dream, invest, create, produce and be of service and you will find there is no limit to your prosperity. Take the time to review your own skills and natural talents and direct them to how you can provide the best service to others and educate yourself on finances and economics, and you will find there is no limit to what you can earn. Financial freedom is not easy but is a worthy and noble cause for all and one you won't regret.

Here are my top ten tips for your financial security:

(1) 70/10/10/10 strategy — a little financial model to get you thinking about how to allocate your money with investing, business, saving and giving, but you could change the allocation to suit your needs and to grow your own wealth:

70% to live on for daily expenses

10% active investment. Buy, sell, invest, rent, create, start a side gig, start or buy a business — use your entrepreneur spirit.

10% passive investment — savings in cash or commodities. Peace of mind for when you lose your job or have an emergency.

10% to donate to charity and give to your choice of providers.

Start this as early as possible to allow the power of compounding interest to work its magic.

(2) Reduce debts. Bad Debt is like being a slave in chains to creditors. Good debt can be helpful to create wealth and use leverage but bad debt is to be avoided at all costs.

(3) Know your balance sheet — know your income/expenses/assets/liabilities.

(4) Focus on positive cashflow — the key to financial independence is that your investments cashflow outweighs your expenses. Once you break free, with more coming in than going out, you become financially independent. That is the secret to financial independence. Building assets and cash-

flow is the name of the game. Business and investments are the main vehicles the rich use to drive wealth and cashflow.

(5) Invest in sound money like gold and silver and other hard assets in highly inflationary periods such as what the world is seeing today. Look for physical items in highly inflationary periods like gold, silver, farmland, art, livestock, commodities and housing, if well priced, to hedge against currency collapse and hyperinflation with real things that are not paper based. This saved people in Argentina, Venezuela, Turkey and Zimbabwe when those currencies collapsed.

Keep educated with the movements in crypto and Bitcoin, which looks to become the people's financial system rather than the banks and government system and is moving at incredible speed in the digital era and becoming more and more attractive to many investors.

(6) Educate yourself on finance and economics and never stop studying and learning finance, as the modern world changes so fast today.

(7) Study history: What has happened has all been seen before. As Churchill says, "The longer you can look back, the farther you can look forward."

(8) Hold twelve months of savings in cash and precious metals to ride out the unexpected — job loss, unexpected emergencies etc. It is peace of mind for times of trouble and allows you time to regroup. It will also allow you to invest after market crashes when assets of various kinds are going cheap.

(9) Diversify your investments and income sources across multiple asset classes - cash, stocks, gold and silver, commodities, crypto, bitcoin, real estate, farmland, fine art, alternate investments, career and business etc.

(10) Improve your skill set and knowledge base to open up more opportunities.

It is also worth never forgetting the other things in life that money can't buy, such as good relationships, good health, peace of mind, a good night's sleep, adventure and other interests.

Good health

*Good health is worth more than all
the money in the world*

Treat your body like a temple
- Jim Rohn

If I was to offer you ten million dollars but you would only live for one more day, would you take it? All of us would of course say no, which confirms that not even all the money in the world can replace good health and the value of life itself.

I have always been active my whole life, playing a variety of sports and engaging in outdoor activities, and this habit and interest from a young age has been one of the greatest blessings in my life for both my mind and body. This habit or routine that I love has become a foundation and structure for my daily schedule.

Obesity has soared in record numbers around the world, as people spend more and more time in front of electronic screens and move their bodies less and less and have poor diets. Not only have obesity rates soared but so have all sorts of mental ailments, from depression and anxiety, with screen addiction and social media leading to a wave of growing mental health issues that continues to rise each year. Study after study show the rise in unhappiness and other mental ailments across society in all Western countries.

One of the best benefits of exercise is not just maintaining good physical strength, which I now think is a bonus we get, but the feeling it provides us when we take the time to do some form of exercise, no matter how small. It's the ultimate drug to pick you up if you are feeling down. You just feel better when you move your body and sweat, and it also clears your mind and provides more clarity and creativity in your mind.

Health goes well beyond just the physical, to both the mental and spiritual, and they must all work in unity for us to receive the whole reward and benefits and to function at our peak.

We need to care for and cultivate all three functions in our lives to win the health battle of mind, body and spirit.

Without good health, we can't live the life we wish to, and no amount of money can replace this.

Make exercise and good health a daily function in your life. You will look, feel and think better for it and radiate positive energy to those who come in contact with you.

Self care

Self care is a habit we all must develop and practise

How can you help anyone if you're a mess?

Renew yourself mentally, physically and emotionally

Looking after yourself is not selfish

We all know life can be stressful, with work, money, relationships, health and worldly issues always arising throughout our lives, so it is essential that we look after ourselves with daily self care practices that can calm and relax us, away from the stresses of the world.

I made it a practice to self care long before it became popular in the media. We should all make it a routine and a habit in our lives.

If we don't practise self care, we open ourselves up to all sorts of negative health and emotional problems, but with good self care, we can sail through the stressful periods of life much more peacefully and calmly.

Self care is nothing more than good habits that are developed and practised that renew you mentally, physically and emotionally.

Good self care habits include exercise, sleep, eating healthily, drinking water and green tea, socialising with friends, spending time in nature, getting some natural vitamin D from the sun, yoga, reading, swimming, having a hot bath or spa, meditation, prayer, playing with the dog, dancing, practising your hobbies, some quiet time alone, listening to your favourite music, appreciating art, practising gratitude, watching a movie or show that relaxes you, listening to or watching something funny, saying no to requests so you are not overwhelmed, going shopping, getting a massage or manicure and anything else that can relax and renew you.

Self care, just like any good habit, can be developed over time and is essential if we are to take the load off our own shoulders and live a calm and less stressful life. Life is not going to get any easier, and our many responsibilities to ourselves and others are not likely to disappear, so we must develop and use good self care practices so we can lighten our load and meet the demands of the day, and, in the process, ensure our own health and protect ourselves from the demands of the world all around us.

Develop your style

Style never goes out of fashion

Clothes make the man
- Erasmus (Adagia 3.1.60)

Fashion reflects who you are

Fashion fades, style is eternal
- Yves Saint Laurent

People will stare. Make it worth their while
- Harry Winston

They say God looks on the inside and people look on the outside, and whilst there is no doubt our character is far more important, people still judge us by our style — the way we dress and look — and this does indeed matter.

If we want to impress a potential partner, land that new job, win over a new client or just look and feel great, we must develop our style and dress and groom well. You only get one shot to make a great first impression, they say.

Style and grooming is important, and we should all take some time to define our personal style and know the basics for both formal and informal wear for all seasons to make a great impression, and how we can look after ourselves with general cleanliness and grooming with things such as beards, shaving, cologne, short nails, haircuts, clothes well fitted, nice breath, clean boots, etc.

Having style makes you look and feel better and is a great confidence booster. Look at famous musicians, movie stars or sports stars. They often dress with real class and make a great impression on others and ooze confidence. But you don't need to be a Hollywood star to look and feel great and make a great impression.

Start by having a well rounded and diverse wardrobe and accessories for all types of events and seasons, both summer and winter, with tailored suits, jeans, socks, gym gear, jackets, sports jackets, pants, collared shirts, white, black and navy casual shirts, shoes, boots, sneakers, hats of different styles, reading glasses, sunglasses, watches, belts, board shorts, home wear, nightwear and workwear. A core set of just a few staple items can be the framework to mix and match from your wardrobe. The minimalist wardrobe with only essentials is what many men have as a wardrobe framework and still make a great impression.

The fedora hat has become the staple of my style, and many people have commented on my hats over the years. You too can build your own style. Some people love jeans, others love the tailored suit, some the signature everyday jacket, some love casual gym wear, some the baseball hat, others the cowboy look with boots, Stetson hat and a cool pair of sun-

Develop your style

glasses. It does not matter as long as you feel comfortable and confident in it.

Start building your wardrobe little by little, that is uniquely your own style, and own it. Don't be afraid of being unique or different, because you are. People will soon begin to notice you, and you will not only look and feel great but begin to display confidence, which will attract more of the good in life to you.

The horsemen of the mind

The horsemen of the mind are the greatest threats to your life

In antiquity, they said the four horsemen of the apocalypse that would end the world were fire, famine, war and death.

Today, we each fight the horsemen of the mind, who will stop at nothing to destroy our lives and dreams. They are the most destructive things you can let into your mind — the killers of your future and the anchors on your ship of progress.

These new horsemen of the mind are fear, greed, ego, envy, worry, revenge, anger and jealousy. If you can fight these off and limit these horsemen of the mind, chances are high that you will live a great and happy life. If a few of these deadly emotions get hold of you, you're going to be in big trouble. History has proven this to be true, from the Bible to Shakespeare. You can prove this to yourself by asking: Who do I know personally whose life has been consumed by these deadly emotions of the mind? It will be very clear that those who fell into hard times or emotional wars would have been consumed by at least one of these deadly emotions.

The horsemen of the mind

These new horsemen are so dangerous that, in fact, they have created wars, killed billions, destroyed countries, broken relationships, sent billions into bankruptcy, stolen from the people, sent people insane, and stolen the happiness and joy from millions. Despite their utter destruction, people can't see or touch these powerful forces, but we all know they are pervasive and how dangerous they really are.

Emotions rule the world, as discussed in an earlier chapter, and we must battle all our living days to not let these ugly emotions take control of our life. It's not going to be easy, and you and I have all fallen to these ugly emotions, which can be relentless in their attacks at one time or another.

We must be aware of the dangers they pose and look to go against the crowd and cultivate positive emotions such as love, freedom, patriotism, hope, generosity, compassion, faith, courage, calmness, commitment, forgiveness, and kindness. These are not emotions that control our lives with chains but provide freedom and clear space in the mind and destroy the other deadly forces that wish to swap places in our mind and will look for any opportunity if we are not careful.

Look to this one day only

Just worry about today's work

Look to this Day is an ancient Sanskrit poem about the importance of a single day and how we should look to this one day only, as it is life, and in its brief course lie all the realities of our existence. The bliss of growth, the glory of action, and the splendour of beauty all lie within that one day alone.

The poem goes on to say: "For yesterday is nothing but a dream and tomorrow is only a vision of what may be, but today well lived makes every yesterday a dream of happiness and tomorrow a vision of hope. Look well to this day for it is all we have."

Sadly, we tend to waste the most important asset we all have, which is time, often on the meaningless and fruitless, and fritter away our days. We then look back with sadness and regret as we finish our lives.

The accumulation of either productive or wasted days can determine what sort of life we have lived when we look back at it. It all starts from looking at this one day only and making the most of it.

The routine of one day does not seem much, but the compound impact over a week, a month, a year, a decade and a lifetime is incredible in its power and reach to mould the lives we desire to live.

Forget about what has been and what may be and just put your focus on using all that you have in this present moment. With it, we can mould, shape and design the lives we want and create and produce memories and experiences we could never have imagined possible. Look to this one day only!

Every morning you come alive again

The past regrets and future fears are washed away every morning

One of life's greatest blessings is that no matter what happens the day or night before or how dark or dire things may be, every morning we come alive again, and often all the fears and worries of the past seem to be gone with a new day. The night before may seem dark, but miraculously, when the sun rises again, we also come alive again. The clouds of the past are now clear blue skies and we are renewed, mentally, physically and spiritually.

It's hard to describe this law, and I would say it is somewhat miraculous how this happens. But work with this law, as, no matter how dark things may be, the promise of a new day and revitalisation and new inspiration will come. You may feel tired, worn out, and that your situation is hopeless, but with a good night's rest, we come alive again and are renewed every morning.

Think on death

Think on death daily

Death is an incredible tool

Live with no regrets

Somebody should tell us, right at the start of our lives, that we are dying. Then we might live life to the limit, every minute of every day
- Michael Lander

A man can die but once. We owe God a death
- Shakespeare (Henry IV, 2, Act III, Scene 2)

One of the most powerful practices I often do is reflect on death. This is counterintuitive to most people, who feel the topic of death is a taboo subject. Death is certain for all and should not be feared, but understood, as it is a part of our earthly experience. Death can be one of the most powerful tools to instruct and help us live a life of higher meaning and purpose, and live with no regrets.

How often do we hear stories about people who reach the end of their lives and regret all sorts of stuff and how they lived? Most of the time it is the things they didn't do rather than the things they did. Death brings to light what is really important and what is not. Those who lose a loved one or face a financial or health crisis quickly come to realise what is important and what is not.

One tool that I have learned is to list all the things I would regret if I died today. This simple tool keeps me on track for what is important and what is not important.

For me, it was travel locations, writing books, reading extensively from many great authors, being generous, being creative and productive, relationships, playing sports and exercising, rugby league, hobbies, music, being of service, becoming more compassionate, and weeding out those character flaws that I have.

Death is an incredibly powerful tool and it can be leveraged for the good and help us live an even better life when we know death is certain and time is short.

We can each live a good or maybe great life and reach the end, no matter when, and have no regrets. Ponder death often to keep at the forefront what is really important and to recognise what is just noise.

Keep bouncing

Never never give in
- Winston Churchill

Success consists of going from failure to failure without loss of enthusiasm
- Winston Churchill

Famous World War Two Leader George Patton told his students and the men under his leadership to always keep bouncing in the face of setbacks, failures and adversity. Patton knew a thing or two about failure. After being in the wilderness for many years, he had to wait a long time for his destiny to be fulfilled. He led the allied forces in World War Two to incredible success, with his army winning battle after battle in Africa, Sicily, and Europe which cemented his legacy forever in the American analogue. He died at the end of the war in a car accident.

Patton talked to his men about Benedict Arnold, who became a traitor to America, George Washington and the American freedom movement in the revolutionary war. Arnold became a traitor to his nation after having incredible success in the war and then, when being overlooked for promotion, jumped to the British side. As Patton says, this could have all been avoided if Arnold knew how to keep bouncing and handle the adversity, rejections and failures better.

Failure, adversity, self doubt, and unexpected emergencies are all part of life, and we are certain to get our fair share. We must keep bouncing through these valleys of life.

We see the talented sportspeople who have all the skills in the world for success, yet they never reach the top. Often the missing characteristic is that they don't have the internal forge or character attributes to go through the fire and keep persisting when things get hard or don't go to plan.

To keep bouncing is not the easiest practice to learn, but we must if we are to become more, have more and be more. This is to persist when there seems no hope, to get up again and again despite the falls and setbacks, to keep going when your friends, family and others mock you, to climb again after a financial, business, career, relationship or health crisis.

Keep bouncing, as Patton says, and know your time will come.

Carry the fire

Are we the good guys?
- Cormac McCarthy

You do your worst and we will do our best

In Cormac McCarthy's acclaimed novel *The Road,* the father and son who are attempting to survive in a post-apocalyptic world continually urge each other to carry the fire in what really is a love story between a father and son, when you look at the core of the novel.

"Carry the fire" has many meanings to readers but really it is a metaphor on how to live!

This line has had a massive impact on many readers, who feel deep-seated emotion to carry the fire in their own lives, doing good whilst evil abounds and remaining one of the good guys, no matter the costs or challenges, as shown in McCarthy's classic story.

We each need to carry the fire in our own lives, the fire to do our best, to do good, to be generous in service and deed and never lose hope, no matter how dire or bleak things may become.

Carry the fire in your own life, and look for reasons that give your life meaning and purpose. Maybe it's work, maybe your family or children, your community, a strong cause, solving a crisis or just being a good person within your community. Without the fire inside us, we become dull and lifeless, and fall prey to all sorts of internal and external threats that aim to stop our progress.

Carry the fire and never let the light go out until your last breath. Pass this attitude on to all who you come in contact with. The burning flame from within can push us through any form of adversity we face and ensure we become the people we were meant to be, and help lift others up through their own struggles, with both example and inspiration.

Follow your own path

Be true to yourself

Know who you are
- Socrates

*Success is a progressive realisation
of a worthy goal or ideal*
- Earl Nightingale

Abraham Lincoln said, "God must have loved the common man because he made so many." He would have been closer to the truth if he'd said, "God must have loved the uncommon man because there are so many about."

Comparing yourself to others is the quickest path to disappointment and unhappiness, as we are neither inferior nor superior but just us, and that is uncommon. We all come with different personalities, skills, temperaments, and traits, and we should cultivate who we are and what we have been given and never try to compare ourselves with others. This is impossible, but millions do this every day.

How often do you see the mother telling one of her two boys to be more like the other brother who may be superior in certain things and inferior in others? But we can never be like others.

Instead of trying to be like others, which we can never achieve, let's cultivate what we have and can be.

Many parents force kids to play sport or go into a career such as law or accounting because the family has a history in this field or because it is expected, but the person may have absolutely no interest in a particular sport or career field.

We are each made different, and the education system, media, and workplaces try to mould us into something we often are not.

Earl Nightingale has the best definition of success I have ever heard: that success is a progressive realisation of a worthy goal or ideal — basically making life what we want it to be and not allowing life to be measured by someone else, even if we do not reach our goal. To Nightingale, if a girl was a mother because that was her most dear wish, that person is a smashing success; if a corporate worker quits his job and heads to the mountains to live a quiet life as he had dreamt about, that person was a smashing success.

Each of us is unique. We must run our own race and become what we desire and not what others want or believe. If we follow another's path, we will live a life of regret, agony and disappointment. Only by following our own path can we find who we really are, as Nietzsche said, becoming who you are.

Epitaph - your legacy

That's what it says
- Augustus Gus McCrae (Lonesome Dove)

*I've seen your father bury many a man, but I
never known him to carve a sign before*
- Gus McCrae on Woodrow F Call's epitaph for Josh Deets
(Lonesome Dove)

You can write whatever you want for your life

How would you like to be remembered?

One of my favourite television series and books is *Lonesome Dove*, the story of two retired Texas rangers who look for one last great adventure in the new frontier before the masses arrive, by moving a large herd of cattle to Montana from Texas with a cohort of characters. The story, which was adapted from Larry McMurtry's novel *Lonesome Dove*, has been described by some as the Cowboy Odyssey from Homer's original Greek novel, *The Odyssey*. Like Homer's great tale, it's an adventure of the unknown, with many twists and turns that have made it a favourite of many readers.

HillBilly: Lessons for the Road

One of the most moving scenes in the series is when Gus McCrae reads the epitaph for Josh Deets, who is killed by Indians. A rock is carved into an epitaph sign by fellow Texas ranger Woodrow F Call. Gus reads out a short emotional and beautiful tribute to their fallen friend after being asked by Pea Eye Parker to read the carved sign.

Pea Eye Parker: *What's it read, Gus?*

Gus McCrae: *It says, "Josh Deets. Served with me 30 years. Fought in 21 engagements with the Comanche and the Kiowa. Cheerful in all weathers. Never shirked a task. Splendid behavior." That's what it says.*

We each die but it is up to each of us what we want written as the epitaph for our life. We each only get one shot at life and we ain't coming this way again. So let's make the best of what we have and be remembered for what we did and gave to others. Forget about the past hurts, regrets and mistakes we have all made. Keep moving forward with great drive and determination, despite the many setbacks and failures, to live the life you have always wanted, and leave a legacy for others to follow.

How do you want to be remembered? What do you want others to say about you once you depart this world?

Epilogue

*It's better to know victory or defeat than the
cold and timid souls that know neither*
- Teddy Roosevelt

*If one advances confidently in the direction of his dreams,
and endeavors to live the life which he has imagined, he
will meet with a success unexpected in common hours*
- Henry David Thoreau

*There is a tide in the affairs of men, which, taken at
the flood, leads on to fortune; omitted, all the voyage
of their life is bound in shallows and in miseries*
- Shakespeare (Julius Caesar, Act IV, Scene 2)

Get busy living or get busy dying
- Shawshank Redemption

If you're like me, which most readers will be, you're probably going to have to go down the long and winding route to achieve what you most desire from life. It's a road filled with challenges and great adversity, even more so in the current global climate, and life will test you like you never expected, but it must be taken if you wish to break free from the world around you and live life on your own terms. Rich parents, luck of the draw or some other miracle didn't come my way and it's probably not going to come your way, so you're going to have to make do with what you have and forge your own path. But that's okay because what you have is enough to get you to where you want to go and who you want to become.

Take some of these lessons and laws and apply them to your life. They are designed to be short and sweet so you can remember them and go back and review these core lessons of each law when needed.

Everything that has ever been and everything that ever will be is here now and can be discovered. You have all the talents and abilities to design the life you have always dreamed of. It's not some pipe dream, so please give yourself a chance. No matter what has happened in the past or where we are today in life, we can all do the incredible from nothing. The stories have proven this throughout the ages! Always remember that all positions in life are temporary and wherever you are is okay, only your direction is critical.

The river of time does not stop flowing, nor does it flow in reverse! You ain't coming this way again, so get at it and make the most of the time you have left. Live with no regrets and design the life you want!

You have the power to mould the life you want. Study this material and go out and make it happen with action.

Life gets better when we get better and become more. When we grow more, our problems become easier to deal with, so focus on becoming more and adding true value, and everything will fall into place, and when problems do arise, your

Epilogue

hand is not short and you have the intelligence, knowledge, characteristics, spirit and capabilities to solve anything.

William E Bailey coined the phrase "Why not you and why not now?" and it is a philosophy I urge you to follow and live out.

Why not you having the adventures available, travelling to amazing countries around the world, being fit and healthy at any age, being extremely generous to others and your community, finding that special someone, cultivating new and old relationships, becoming more valuable and knowledgeable, becoming a person of virtue, gaining financial freedom and performing work that you enjoy and taking pride in it, giving you great inner satisfaction?

Why not now? There is no better time and you ain't coming this way again, so get at it.

I wish you peace, health, wealth, wisdom, friendships, happiness and adventure for your life.

May you travel the road that leads to your destiny being fulfilled.

Billy Roberts

www.ingramcontent.com/pod-product-compliance
Lightning Source LLC
Chambersburg PA
CBHW031235290426
44109CB00012B/310